2003
Nurturing
for Community

MW01004853

DATE DUE

248.8
M

surprisedbychildren

Todd   Greg   Rick   Andy
Lisa   Jeanette   Harold   Michelle
    Joshua   Lindsey

one man's embrace
of fatherhood...again

surprisedbychildren
a memoir

harold myra

ZondervanPublishingHouse
Grand Rapids, Michigan

A Division of HarperCollins*Publishers*

Surprised by Children
Copyright © 2001 by Harold L. Myra

Requests for information should be addressed to:

ZondervanPublishingHouse
Grand Rapids, Michigan 49530

Library of Congress Cataloging-in-Publication Data
Myra, Harold Lawrence, 1939-
 Surprised by children / Harold Myra.
  p. cm.
 ISBN: 0-310-23465-4
 1. Christian biography. 2. Myra, Harold Lawrence, 1939- 3. Fatherhood—Religious
aspects—Christianity. 4. Fatherhood—Religious aspects—Christianity. I. Title.
BR1700.2 .M97 2001
248.8'45'092—dc21   00-051291
[B}   CIP

This edition is printed on acid-free paper.

Some names have been changed to protect privacy.

Interior design by Todd Sprague

Printed in the United States of America

01 02 03 04 05 06 /❖ DC/ 10 9 8 7 6 5 4 3 2 1

sprawled on the floor

*A*s I flip through notes and photos to start this book, images of children dance in my head. I am thinking, *What a careening ride these kids have taken me on.* Though I haven't been dodging bullets or dangling from rooftops, I feel I've been living out a wild adventure—a quirky, mysterious, humbling adventure.

I grab a legal pad to scratch out ideas, but Lindsey, four and a half years old, prances into my den. Soon she has me pulled from my desk and sprawled on the floor beside her as she uses a Magic Marker to color a cat yellow and blue. A beautiful child, red-and-yellow beads dangling in braids on her cheeks, she grabs my hand, her lovely brown fingers gripping my white wrist.

Suddenly she stands up with a huge smile, pulls me up beside her, and begins whirling around me, round and round, singing, "I love you, Daddy. I love you and I always will. I love you, Daddy."

As she dances, I think that this is like some dream from a Pollyanna movie. She looks into my face and says, "I love it when you're around, Daddy!" She opens her arms wide, stretching them out like a bird. "I'll give you a *big* hug." She flings her arms around me, saying, "I love you *so* much!"

The night before as I told her good night, I added, "You're really fun."

"No, Daddy," she had insisted with adult authority, "you're the fun one!" She corrected me in such a definite and lovable way, I couldn't hold back my laughter.

Lindsey dances out of the room and down the hall, and I smile. But as I think about how I became her dad, and all the turmoil of young lives that's washed over my wife, Jeanette, and me, it doesn't feel like *Pollyanna.*

More like *The Hobbit,* in which Bilbo Baggins battles giant spiders, faces a flaming dragon, and day after day treks a lightless forest, with little hope—but then finds he's wonderfully changed everything.

My pen dawdles on the pad. I think of the Narnia children and Tolkien's hobbits. Is my journey like theirs?

After all Bilbo's escapades, the wizard Gandalf said to him, "You don't really suppose, do you, that all your adventures . . . were managed by mere luck, just for your sole benefit? You are a very fine person, Mr. Baggins, and I am very fond of you; but you are only quite a little fellow in a wide world after all."

Bilbo responded, laughing, "Thank goodness."

So here I am, a little fellow in a world more supernatural than usually thought. Maybe that's why I'm writing this book—to see what God has been up to in all this. To step back and try to glimpse what's truly going on in these adventures with children.

From the bedroom next door come computer sounds of the *Lego Island* game. I leave the pen on the pad and find at the computer six-year-old Joshua and ten-year-old Rick maneuvering a Lego boy on a skateboard as he delivers pizza on the island.

Suddenly Josh jumps off his chair and breaks into the hall for some impromptu gymnastics. He's a natural—a flying, flipping little ball. "Come here, Josh!" As I lift him, he gives me a strong, tight hug and a big, infectious smile.

Rick too has an infectious smile. I watch him expertly roar around Lego Island; already he knows more about computers than his dad. As he plays, I grin as I remember a day four years ago when I accidentally called him his brother's name. "Oops. Sorry, Rick," I'd said with a grin. "One of these days I have to get my brain fixed."

A few days later little Rick had come up to me and very seriously asked, "Dad, when are you going to get your brain fixed?" He wondered why I laughed so hard, but he laughed with me. He'd assumed it was like scheduling a dentist appointment and had believed my words exactly.

A year before, he had wanted to go on an errand with me. I said, "You wouldn't like it. You'd be bored."

Rick had looked up at me and said, "I'll go wherever you go, Dad."

Weighty implications. But now as I watch this preteen, who's heavily into soccer, basketball, and friendships, I realize that the window of his listening to me and following me is narrowing.

Lindsey, Josh, Rick. Three remarkable lives that amaze and sober me, bless me yet stress me out.

Back in my den the notepad is empty. How do I start? The publisher who first urged me to write about our children said, "Simply tell the tales." An editor later said, "Yes, tell the stories, but tell your story too. We must see this through your eyes. Why did you respond to these children? What shaped you? What made you respond as you did?"

Those questions take me back to Camden, New Jersey, and a conversation with a cab driver which showed the irony of my having black children and my being born there.

I had just landed at Philadelphia's airport and had stepped into a cab. The African-American driver followed the loop toward the city, accelerating up the long bridge that stretches above the smokestacks. Ships lay in the water, and I wondered if I was seeing the shipyards in which my father worked during World War II.

"I was born in Camden," I said. "In Cooper Hospital."

"Camden?" he exclaimed. "Camden! That's a terrible place. I'd *never* drive over there."

I was startled. Camden was just over the river. Could it be that dangerous for him to drive into my boyhood community?

Later I read a *Time* magazine cover story on Camden that described black poverty, hunger, gangs, and death. It said that in Cooper Hospital now, babies enter the world severely damaged by drugs and neglect. But when I was born in 1939, Camden's families, both black and white, were intact and stable.

My eyes go to shelves full of books and articles about our country's racial tragedies. I feel the tug to start this book with chapters on why so much has changed since 1939, yet so little—and why race continues to bitterly divide us and why thousands of beautiful black children have no homes.

But Joshua cartwheels down the hall outside my door. I hear the thump, thump, thump of Rick dribbling his basketball on the driveway. No, I think, not history and analysis. I need to "just tell the story," starting with Camden when the whole world was accelerating into war.

chapter one

"**W**hat are those for?" my older brother asked as air-raid sirens suddenly blared.

Mother immediately turned off the kitchen lights, then quickly entered the living room, where I sat with scissors and crayons. I looked at the window; everything was dark. "Don't worry," Mother said, reaching for another switch. "This is just a practice."

Click, click, click. Suddenly it was dark all around me. The war for the first time seemed very personal.

Mother had told us more than once how shocked she had been when she had heard President Roosevelt's voice on the radio announcing that the Japanese, in a "day that will live in infamy," had bombed Pearl Harbor. Now I was listening to sirens and thinking about the pictures in my room of Japanese Zeros and German fighters shooting at Allied planes. Doolittle's raiders had bombed Japan; were they now retaliating? Would they bomb the shipyards where Dad worked? Might the bombs hit us?

"What if someone leaves the lights on?" I asked.

"They're not supposed to," Mother said. "But don't worry. It's just a practice."

After what seemed a very long time, Mother turned the lights back on. I blinked in the light, but my mind was still full of exploding bombs and the blunt shapes of Japanese bombers somewhere above Camden and our house.

The war affected all of us. Dad became a fitter for navy ships. Mother's cousins, Tommy and Ralph, joined the military. Rationing was imposed. News and talk of the war were everywhere.

I searched the streets for empty cigarette packs, peeled off the thin aluminum inside, and tried to build the foils into a big ball "for the war effort." Supposedly, it would be worth fifty cents, but I never got a ball big enough. Our trips to visit relatives were on baloney-skin tires that had to be patched and repatched en route.

We boys were strongly patriotic. A photo of my brother and me with a neighbor girl shows us smartly saluting the American flag in front of our pup tent.

But one day the war ended. Suddenly the word was flying from mouth to mouth that we had won. Everyone was shouting that the war was over, and I was marching behind my brother and other children, all of us banging on trash-can lids and shouting as loudly as possible: "The war is over! We won!" To every passing car, we held up our fingers like Churchill in a V for victory. Adults exultantly gave the sign back to us. I felt like an adult myself, swept up in exuberant celebration.

The war that had started when I was born was finally over!

Camden back in those energetic war days was, in the words of *Time,* a city of "gusto and grit," the home of Campbell's soups and Esterbrook pens. "Bard of it all was Walt Whitman, whose spirit trembled at the call of an industrial giant that thrived on the energy, poetry and power of machines."

Both of my parents became part of that optimistic spirit, working hard and building for the future. Yet they were also marked by the past.

My father had immigrated from Norway with his mother when he was seventeen, and he had explored the West in a Model T as far as Idaho. But by the time he met my mother, the Depression had hit.

When Mother's parents had come from Norway, they had met with hard times. Their first two baby girls died; years later, during the Depression, Mother would watch her skilled carpenter father come home after long days on the streets trying to sell locks door-to-door. He would empty his pockets on the kitchen table, revealing odds and ends but not one nickel.

Mother worked in Philadelphia factories in her mid-teens and later sixty hours per week at a dentist's office for $5.00 per week (it cost her $2.50 per week for carfare and a small lunch). After the war we felt the times getting better, yet we remembered the Depression, and we were still relatively poor. My only trike was a wretched hand-me-down that once punctured my calf with an oily wire; later my only bike was a lopsided, mostly useless thing my brother had pulled out of a trash can. Yet none of that mattered much.

Life was uncomplicated. We played mumblety-peg with old knives, arcing them deftly into the dirt. We shinnied up poles and trees and scrounged up old hoses to cut into eight-inch lengths for stickball in the streets. In the evenings we listened to *The Green Hornet* and *The Shadow* on the radio.

Boys I knew delighted in all sorts of mischief: systematically shooting out all the streetlights with BB guns; stealing boxes of railroad flares and setting them off; lighting fires in fields so fire trucks would arrive with blaring sirens and lights, and then helping put the fires out.

However, community and family kept us from dire consequences. Only once did I get into major trouble myself.

I was a first-grader, and I had a nickel. To my older brother, Johnny and his friend Earl, this was irresistible opportunity. They hounded me, saying how fabulous it was that I had a nickel, and just think how many matches that could buy. I resisted a long time, hanging on to my nickel—but eventually gave in.

Back then you could buy a package of eight matchboxes for a nickel. As soon as we were out of the store, Earl ripped a box out of the wrapper, struck a match, and tossed it into dry grass beside the sidewalk. It flamed up.

Johnny and I stared at this phenomenon; then we jumped into the burning grass and stamped the fire out.

Earl had found a new game. He started tossing lighted matches into each clump of grass as he walked along. Johnny and I jumped on the little fires, angrily stamping them out, telling Earl to quit it.

This went on and on. By this time we were yelling at Earl, but he refused to quit. He loved this new game. He kept throwing matches for two long blocks.

Johnny and I stamped out fire after fire after fire. Or at least we thought we had. About four blocks away we heard fire engines.

A moment later a woman ran up to us. "I saw you! It's you kids that set that fire!" She glared at us. "Where are the matches?"

Earl was standing hunched a little forward, the package of match-boxes making an obvious bulge under his shirt.

"What matches? We don't have any matches."

The woman angrily yanked Earl's shirt back, grabbed the boxes, and marched the two older boys back toward the fire engines. I fled home.

Next morning as I sat in my first-grade class, the teacher spoke the dreadful words: "Harold, you are wanted in the principal's office."

Led down long corridors, I entered the wood-paneled office, where Johnny sat glum-faced. There stood not only the principal but a uniformed police officer. After getting our confessions, the police-man led us outside to his squad car. Then he drove us home to the sure discipline of my father.

We knew our boundaries even as we pushed them. Instead of urban hostility toward police, we saw them as stern but fair and in league with our parents.

For instance, in winter snows we would "hop" passing cars. It was absurdly dangerous. Grasping our sleds, we would run beside a car as fast as we could, then belly flop and grab the extended back bumper, hanging on for dear life. Once Johnny found out I had hopped a cop's car. "You can't do that!" he told me. "He'll put you in jail."

But I felt proud of the feat. "He won't," I said. "He's our neighbor." And indeed he lived next door. My only fear was that he might report it to my mother.

Yet I had other fears. Fighting was part of being male, and getting beat up was the risk of walking back and forth to school. One day I watched Francis, a quiet Catholic kid with freckles and very red hair, stand up to a bully who promptly punched him in the nose. His face was quickly splattered with blood that matched his hair.

It was best to stick with my big brother, Johnny. One day as several of us walked home, a boy told us a classmate had a TV in his house. "He'll let us in. Come on!"

I had never seen a TV or, for that matter, a movie or cartoon. I eagerly followed the boys as they rushed down the street and entered a house.

We crowded into the living room, eyes instantly riveted on the lighted screen, where cowboys were arguing in a saloon. A desperado grabbed a bottle, smashed it against the bar, and then lurched toward a clean-cut cowboy. The cowboy dodged and hit the man in the jaw. Bottles, fists, and bodies flew over and under the bar. Then the fighters battled up the stairs and out onto an upper-story porch. A big, beefy outlaw struck the cowboy in the chest, smashing him into the railing, which split, swayed, and fell, dropping the hero onto the street below.

My brother's hand pulled on my shirt. "We've got to go."

What? Not yet! I had to see more. The action had blazed into me, churning my emotions, transporting me into an alternate world.

I stepped onto the sidewalk astounded and fascinated by this new experience. Yet in some ways, the new TV world in which men smashed bottles and each other was not new to me at all. In a world of war and bullies, it simply escalated reality.

I knew that life could be dangerous and that it was foolish to wander out of my own territory. Who knew what might happen out there among strangers?

The Acres near our home was an apartment complex; beyond those buildings lived African-Americans. Yet I had never seen a black kid in our school. I knew some must live in Camden, for we were all proud that Jersey Joe Walcott, the black boxer, was from our city.

Once Johnny's teacher asked a boy in his class to take a note after school to the black neighborhood. The boy refused. She asked another boy and he too said no. Then she asked Johnny to do it.

Johnny was on the spot. He could also refuse and show his fear as the other boys had. Or he could say yes and walk from school past the

Acres to a neighborhood he'd never entered before and risk who knew what.

His reputation was on the line; he swallowed and told the teacher he'd do it. After school he delivered the note.

Nothing at all happened to him.

Yet tough white kids could be ruthless. One afternoon Johnny and I were walking home from school when we suddenly found ourselves surrounded by four older boys we didn't know. Johnny was a good fighter, but they pushed us into a field, threw ropes around us, and shoved us down on the ground.

"What did we do?" we demanded. "We didn't do anything to you."

They laughed, tying us up, tangling us together, cinching the knots tight. They thoroughly enjoyed themselves, taunting us and pulling on the ropes.

Then the bullies left us in the secluded field—just left us trussed up. We yelled at them to free us but they were soon gone.

At first a wave of relief rolled over me. They're gone! Now we can squirm free. We yanked at the ropes, thinking we could surely get loose somehow. But we couldn't. We strained and strained, feeling panic building as it started getting dark.

We lay there as the light slowly vanished. The moon and stars appeared. We wondered how anyone could find us in the dark and how long this could go on.

At long, long last, under the evening sky, we heard our father's voice. He had searched all along the way to school and found us in the field.

My dad loved me with quiet support and thoughtfulness. My mother loved me with a kind of beautiful irrationality. Her love was the air I breathed, the energy of life. Once in third grade I walked down the aisle of the school auditorium, students to my left and right, with this soaring feeling that I could do anything at all I decided to do, that it was a remarkable secret only I of all these students knew. That feeling came from my mother, and from her God.

Her moral clarity shaped me. For instance, I was about five the day I sat on the sidewalk with other children in front of a neighborhood store. We were chanting, "Don't buy at Abbie's! Don't buy at Abbie's!" We banged on cans and sang the little ditty over and over.

I had no idea why we were singing the jingle, but its naughty flavor must have broken up the boredom. We chanted and banged, staring at the store's front door, ready to run if "Abbie"—whoever that was—came out.

I then rode my trike the two blocks home and played in the backyard. But that night Mother found out about the chants and was furious. She ordered us to stop and she quoted the Bible to us. I knew nothing about Jewishness or anti-Semitism, but I learned in no uncertain terms that she wouldn't tolerate this behavior.

"Pastor Bauer says the Bible is very clear," she said. "'He who curses the Jews is cursed; he who blesses them is blessed.'"

Mother took her Bible very seriously. One day at school, on my way to meet her I bounded past the polio victims on the landing of the stairs. When she saw me coming, she smiled, then asked, "Did you see those children with polio?"

I looked back at an older boy, legs splayed out in steel braces, and two girls with metal contraptions supporting their bodies. "Yes," I said. "I see them." But I hadn't really seen them.

As we drove home, Mother said, "I feel so very sorry for those children. Think how you would feel. One day you're just like other kids, and then you go swimming and get sick, and suddenly you're never able to swim again, or walk. . . ."

She also made sure we attended church and in the summer, Pinebrook Bible Conference in the Pocono Mountains of Pennsylvania. In fact, she and Dad were so taken with the Poconos and the chance for a rural life that by 1948 they decided we should move there.

chapter two

Several years after our move from Camden to the Poconos, I was abruptly blindsided by prejudice. Our short yellow school bus came to a stop at the village of Delaware Water Gap. A little brother and sister—first-graders, I guessed—got on the bus for the first time. Cute kids, I thought.

I forgot about the newcomers until they boarded the bus again after school. On the way home I heard a commotion at the front of the bus. A big, burly seventh-grader named Joe had been saying something to the smaller children, and as they got off, they were crying. Joe was often crude, and I figured he had been calling them names, but I didn't really get what was going on.

The next day on the return trip from school, we stopped again at Delaware Water Gap. As soon as the kindly, quiet bus driver opened the doors to let the tots off, their Jewish mother climbed up the bus stairs in a fury and accosted him. She shouted that what had happened to her children was despicable. "They will never ride this school bus again! Never, never, never!" Then she escorted her children off the bus and stormed away with them.

I was stunned. While she was shouting at the driver, I had finally figured it out. I suddenly wanted to do something and started to get out of my seat. I wanted to shout out the window to the mother, "*No! Let your children come again tomorrow. Not everyone is like that! You've got to let them come again. I'll stand up for your little girl and your little boy!*"

But the windows were closed. The bus was already moving, turning and starting its ascent up the mountain while the woman was striding angrily away, a child's hand in each of hers.

I sat dumbfounded. Inside I was screaming, "I didn't know! I didn't know!" How had that happened without my seeing—really seeing?

I never saw the children again. For a long time I was angry at myself, not for having failed to stand up to the bully but for having been unaware. It became a personal illustration to me of how ignorance keeps one from doing the right thing.

Yet I was at least grateful for my instinct to protest—not because of any goodness on my part but simply because this is what I had been taught. While Nazi Germany, with its Lutheran heritage, was exterminating Jews, my mother had learned in St. Paul's Lutheran Church in Camden that "he who blesses the Jews will be blessed."

If today's kids live in a world of *Star Wars* and interplanetary adventure, in the 1950s our world was the West. Heroes were tall in the saddle and lived by a clear code. John Wayne might have had rough edges, but he knew who he was and how to overcome impossible odds. To my brother and me, our identity was fused with the men of steely honor who defended it with a Winchester or Colt .45.

Guns were common in the Poconos. In eighth grade on the first day of deer season, only girls went to school. A boy showing up would have been disgraced. I have a photo of myself as a high school sophomore holding a .30–30 Winchester, wearing my cartridge belt and pistol, the head of my five-point buck propped up against my leg. The pose is heroic, like any Zane Grey hero, face against the wind.

I wore that .22 pistol, with its western holster tied down, every time I walked the woods. It was essential garb. Once while walking along the road near the house, my brother in one of his more reckless moments fired a shot that ricocheted off the hard dirt somewhere in my vicinity. In reaction I found myself lying flat on my belly, my pistol drawn and aimed at him, my left hand steadying my right. My conscious mind had not put me into that position; mine was automatic reflex, so total was my identity with the western hero.

African-Americans did not exist in that world.

While the Brooklyn Dodgers I rooted for had Jackie Robinson and Roy Campanella, the cowboy movies and books never depicted a black man in a saddle. United Airlines' magazine once ran an article on Paul Stewart, a black man who, like me, grew up in the time when young men emulated cowboys. He and his friends played cowboys and Indians, but he was never allowed to be a cowboy, even though that's what he longed to be. Since he was black, he was always told he had to be an Indian.

When he grew up, he discovered that many black men had gone to the Old West to carve out new lives. Researching the subject, he found plenty of old newspaper stories showing that a high percentage of the cowboys who won the West were black. More than thirty-five thousand artifacts and photos of black cowboys can be seen in his Black American West Museum in Denver.

In my closet is a complete collection of Zane Grey comic books and dozens of original *Lone Rangers*, *Western Roundups*, and others, tall stacks of them. You could look long and hard through them, but you wouldn't find even one black cowboy.

When racial issues came up in our family, as with many other issues, complexities were unexplored. We did not have spirited exchanges about articles in thought magazines; instead we affirmed Christian verities. Yes, we said, it was sad the way people were treated. Yes, it was terrible what happened in this world. We needed to show love to all and live out our faith.

Though the dialogue was simple, its effect was profound, especially since I felt like a full participant. From my earliest memories, I sensed that whatever Johnny or I said at the dinner table had equal weight with words from Mom or Dad. Lines of authority were clear but our opinions were respected. I felt in those post-Depression years like one of four responsible persons in the family. When I would caddie in the summer, I'd dump all my earnings on the kitchen table.

One morning I was standing between the sink and the stove, making my usual breakfast of eggs and toast. Dad walked in and questioned a judgment call I had made.

I scooped the eggs out of the sizzling bacon fat and flipped them onto my plate. Then I said, "But, Dad, I thought you and Mom told me that when I was fourteen, I was raised—that I could make my own decisions."

He hesitated. Then came his remarkable response, which still amazes me. He broke into a cheerful grin. "You know, you're right!" he said. "You're absolutely right. You are fourteen."

From then on Dad treated me as an adult, and Mom pretty much did the same. Of course, I wasn't making a lot of bad choices, and when decisions like joining the Marine Corps Reserves came along, I wanted their counsel and support. Especially since I was only seventeen and Mom had to sign the permission forms.

Late one evening while still in high school, I sped our family car up our dirt driveway and braked to a stop, still amazed at what I had in the trunk. As I lifted the lid and grabbed my new Marine Corps seabag, I felt a bit the way I had two years before when I'd dragged home that five-point buck. Both seemed trophies of manhood.

However, this trophy in my arms, this big, bulging green bag I was lifting onto my shoulder, was jammed with gear that indeed would initiate me into a man's world. I had joined the Corps because, subject to the draft, I'd wanted to choose a service in which I could take pride. Yet as I carried the bag past the kitchen table and up the stairs, I felt both pride and apprehension. The Marine Corps would be a far bigger challenge than trigonometry and literature classes.

"Want to see?" I asked Mom as I dropped the bag with a thud in the hall between the bedrooms.

"Sure."

I opened it and tipped it over on its side. "Here's the khaki uniform," I said, pulling out a shirt, pants, tie, a narrow garrison cap, then the round barracks cap with the black bill. "Here are the insignias for the collars and caps." My fingers were placing eagle, globe, and anchor on the coarse but dressy material.

Mom was always interested in anything I shared, but her smile was faint.

Was it the brown uniform that bothered her? It was the same color as the uniforms of the young soldiers we'd watched getting on the train for Korea just a few years before. Our family had been shopping in a store across from the train station in East Stroudsburg. We'd been startled to see hundreds of young soldiers on the street. We watched as they came to attention, then filed out row by row to the waiting train.

To me it was a fascinating spectacle, but when I had looked at my mother, I'd seen tears. She pulled me aside. "Harold, those young men are just boys, and they are going to experience terrible things in Korea. I feel so very, very sorry for them." Sobered, I had stared at their receding backs.

Mom watched as out of my bag came two sets of fatigues, black boots, gloves, trench coat, cartridge belt, bayonet. "This goes on the end of the rifle," I said, unable to resist describing its use as I hefted the weapon, knowing she'd rather hear nothing about it.

The first year we had moved up to the Poconos, Dad had to chop the heads off some chickens. Mom had taken me down the road, saying she didn't want me to have to watch. Yet now she was being a good sport, trying to show enthusiasm as I emptied my seabag down to the last shoe. She knew the nation was not at war. Years ago Tommy and Ralph had put on uniforms but had come back. Yes, her sister-in-law's brother at nineteen had been killed at Iwo Jima, but hopefully none of that would happen again.

Yet her weak smile couldn't mask her mixed feelings about her boy handling the instruments of war.

The truth is, Mom and I talked about everything. War. Churches. Marital roles. Her parents' dying. But especially we talked about children: how to love and care for them and not be stupid about what they really needed.

So not long after I started college, while still serving in the Marine Reserves, I wasn't surprised to hear she was considering foster care. "I heard," she said as we sat at the kitchen table, "that they have a huge need for foster parents. Now that you and Johnny are raised, I have the time."

I nodded, swallowing some coffee. Mom had worked either part-time or full-time most of my life, but that no longer seemed necessary. My tuition at the state college nearby was $144 per year; we lived very simply. At a shoe factory she was paid "per piece" and had quintupled her speed and thereby quintupled her pay. But that was only money. Who needed that alongside helping destitute children?

"I've prayed about it," she said. "I've called the state agency."

Not long afterward we sat again at the kitchen table. "We're getting two little boys," she said, "about six and two. The little one's retarded." Mother pursed her lips. "Maybe for no good reason. The neighbors say he might have been fine if he hadn't been left alone in his crib all day." She grimaced with her isn't-the-world-awful look. "Who knows what caused it? Poor little boy. His name is Royal."

Then she told me about his six-year-old brother, Richie. "Can you imagine this? His father told him that if another kid in the neighborhood gave him trouble, 'You just pick up a big rock and you throw it at him as hard as you can!'" She slowly shook her head, both in amazement and perhaps dread of what this boy might bring. "Can you imagine a father saying that?"

"No. That's awful."

"Five kids—three girls and two boys. Sad! Parents never married, and now they've left the state."

Richie and Royal arrived in a nondescript sedan driven by a caseworker. Each had just a small suitcase. They stood awkward and tiny beside the car. Little Royal was blond, eager to please, wide-eyed. Richie had dark hair, pale skin, and an anxious look.

While Mom and Dad talked to the caseworker, I was elected to walk the boys around.

I pointed out our old basketball hoop on an apple tree, and the remains of a tree house Johnny and I had made. A long stone's throw away was my deceased grandparents' empty house trailer and home.

Although we had never planted grass seed, we had a huge lawn, created by simply attacking a fieldful of weeds with a lawn mower. We walked over the grass, past Mom's garden, and toward an empty cinder-block building. "This was the goat barn," I said, shoving open the door. I showed them how the goats would go out to the field I'd fenced in and how I had milked them twice each day. We walked past our ramshackle shed and outhouse to the long rows of empty rabbit hutches.

Richie was polite but cautious, Royal quiet. We were hopeful they would thrive here just as Johnny and I had.

chapter three

While I was still in high school, Youth for Christ came to town. This dynamic movement—of which Billy Graham had been the first staff member—brought upbeat music, humor, and great urgency about reaching kids with the gospel. Confronted with this compelling vision, I vowed to make every moment count for Christ.

During my senior year dozens of us drove to Billy Graham's 1957 New York crusade in Madison Square Garden. After Billy preached, during the invitation I hunched over and prayed so intently for people making decisions that an adult came behind me and touched my shoulder. "Do you want to go forward?" he asked. Slightly embarrassed, I mumbled that I was "just praying."

Hundreds walked forward to receive Christ, and my friends and I were among the last to move toward our cars. We were standing outside the nearly deserted Garden when we saw a half block away a small group of men moving rapidly toward a car.

"Isn't that him?" my friend Marshall suddenly demanded.

"I'm not sure."

"It is! That's Billy!"

In a moment the men were gone. We looked at each other. Yes! We had seen Billy Graham in person!

By the time I started my freshman year at college, I was spending most of my time with YFC. I liked college and got good grades, but for me the real action was reaching kids with the gospel. Each week my beat-up '49 Plymouth carried me to a half dozen Pocono high schools to meet with clubs. As I'd drive the rural roads, I'd think of God's challenge from Jeremiah 33:3: "Call unto me, and I will answer thee, and show thee great and mighty things, which thou knowest not" (KJV).

Great and mighty things. It seemed so to me. One year I traveled thirty-two hours by bus to Kansas City to attend the YFC directors' school. In the summer it was the Ocean City, New Jersey, conference with thousands of high schoolers. Capital Teen Convention in Washington, D.C., drew more than ten thousand teens, with hundreds coming forward at the invitations. All-night prayer meetings, evangelistic rallies, club activities—nothing seemed more important than reaching youth for Christ. Prayer among the leadership was intense, open, powerful—the engine driving it all.

Racial issues still were not on my radar. This was the late fifties and early sixties, before the civil rights movement, when Sputnik, the Cold War, and nuclear annihilation loomed large.

But one day my ignorance and apathy got a jolt. Blond, pretty Rebecca was a regular attender at a YFC club. She was small-boned and so fair, she might have been a poster girl for Icelandic Airways.

One afternoon after a special event, my car was filled with the usual group of teenagers. I dropped them off at their homes one by one until the only one left in the car was Becky. I had never been to her home, but I knew her general neighborhood and headed there.

At the first intersection she said, "Just let me off here."

"Why?" I asked. "Aren't you going home?"

"Yes, but let me off here. This is real close."

I wanted to be kind to her and to let her know she was important enough to take all the way home. "Becky, it's no trouble. Where do you live?"

"Just a couple blocks. This is good enough. Just let me off here."

Foolishly I insisted that I take her all the way home, asking directions as we went.

I still see in my mind's eye the scene as I rounded the last corner and pulled up in front of her small, tan house. It was a little shabby, but I concluded that this wasn't what Becky was afraid I'd see. In the front yard were two little boys, obviously biracial, with bushy hair framing their heads.

"Is this your house?"

"Yes," she mumbled, acting very strange and then departing quickly, scurrying past the little boys, her blond hair and white skin disappearing from the driveway.

I was as dumbfounded as I had been on the bus with the Jewish children. Previously I'd never thought about the fact that her blond hair was frizzy. Now I saw that it matched the hair of the boys in her yard. Were they her younger brothers? Had she been born more white-skinned than they?

Although later I inquired several times about Becky and why she didn't come to club anymore, I never saw her again.

I had learned in college that if you were mostly white and one part black, you were classified as all black, but I had done little thinking about it. Most of us didn't see the outrageousness of using classifications to oppress people of color. I had no concept of the struggles of light-skinned persons of mixed race trying to "pass" into mainstream America, and the resentments from both races at their attempts. Back then, separate seemed just fine to most of us. We didn't see what it was like to live in black skin.

Yet once in a while the truth would hit me. In our college library I picked up a book on the Negro experience and was suddenly sickened at the sight of a photograph of a lynching. In the foreground was a crowd of whites standing around like men and children at a county fair. A few of them were looking at the dangling body of the young man who had been hanged. I wanted to avert my eyes, blank out this monstrous scene. But the dead face of the black boy—he couldn't have been older than I was—forced me to look . . . and to think. What could he have done to madden the mob? How could all those whites simply let that happen and then smile about it? What had it done to the friends and loved ones of this boy?

Another experience, this one in the Marine Corps, stirred up different kinds of questions. Marine boot camp is well known as the ultimate harrowing rite of passage for young men. Drill instructors—DIs—yell at you the instant you get off the bus and keep you running through obstacle courses, bayonet training, twenty-mile hikes with full packs, studying and being tested, firing on the rifle range.

Boot camp for me was the officer candidate version. Our company of about fifty college students was all white, including the DIs. Several times, though, I saw a black DI from another company shouting nose to nose at the only black candidate in his outfit. "You want to be an officer?" he would scream into his face.

"Yes, sir!"

The DI would then grunt in disgust and order the black kid to run flat out. Every time I saw the two of them, the DI was harassing him, running beside him, yelling that he was in no way officer material. It was obvious that the candidate had been singled out because he was black.

I wondered what the DI was trying to prove. Had he been told to do this? Did he believe that this candidate would have to withstand horrendous pressure as a black officer and therefore had to be pushed to the edge? Marine boot camp was supposedly meant to break you if you were breakable, so you wouldn't break later in actual combat. Was that the program here?

It seemed terribly unfair that this student aspiring to be a marine officer would be so mercilessly hounded. Had the DI signaled him that he was testing him for his own good? Or did he hate this young guy? What was going on between these two black men?

I had signed up for the officer program because war then seemed inevitable. I figured I might as well be an officer, yet I also thought about the fabled shortness of a second lieutenant's life expectancy in combat. I often imagined slogging through jungles in Laos waiting for a bullet.

On reserve weekends I would lead the marine worship service; I held on tightly to my faith despite the temptations. But I struggled with the strange juxtaposition of my obeying God yet learning to kill efficiently and even ferociously.

In bayonet training we would run and scream "Kill, kill, kill!" at our fellow marines, our bayonets aimed at each other's guts. Jesus' commands to love our enemies clashed with his blessings on soldiers and with Old Testament tales of warfare for God's sake. How did all this fit?

One night during summer training I waited on the deck of a navy ship, our company preparing to land on a "hostile" beach in the morning. I remembered my aunt's brother at nineteen hitting the beach at Iwo Jima and getting killed on that island. Now I was nineteen, training for just such a moment. The night was clear and the half-moon bright. I could have been looking at the same moon half a world away and been adjusting my gear to face the real thing.

I thought of those young men in uniform about to board the train in East Stroudsburg. More than fifty thousand had died in Korea; some had been horribly tortured. It could happen to me.

Next morning hundreds of us with rifles and packs began descending the nets on the side of the ship. I thought, *Isn't this just like all those war movies and* Victory at Sea *episodes? Marines awkwardly stepping into those little landing craft bobbing on the waves, then riding numbly into white-plumed explosions?*

In the distance high-powered boats circled neatly in groups of four. With perfect precision one would roar out of the circle toward us, followed by the three others. Soon scores of them had been loaded up with us marines.

It was a beautiful day as we rode the landing craft to the beach, gripping our rifles. The boat hit the sand and the gate fell open. Sergeants yelled to move out. I scrambled as fast as I could over the sand toward the brush by the woods. Machine gun fire exploded in front of us but the sergeants yelled to keep moving!

I saw "enemy" marines barely concealed in the woods firing machine guns point-blank at us. We kept running at them but knew that if those were real bullets, we'd be crawling on our bellies. We crashed past them and noisily stumbled through the underbrush. Soon we had "secured the area" and the training exercise was done. But I knew how full of bullet holes I would have been if it had been real.

In the Marine Corps you didn't flinch from what you had to do. Marines died; civilians died; the facts of life were grim. Orders came from above, and you did your part without worrying about personal comfort or survival.

The world was full of tragedy. The Bible said that to whom much was given, much would be required. You did what you had to do in life, whether picking up a rifle or taking in foster kids.

Mom looked to me as well as to Dad for help in parenting Richie and Royal. That was fine with me, and one night when we were alone, Mom asked, "Do you know anything about Dad's watch?"

"Which one?"

"The gold one he brought from Norway. It's very special to him and it's missing. We've been looking everywhere."

I asked her where it had been, and she said it was in the same drawer as always. We talked about various possibilities; then she said soberly, "I think Richie took it."

"Really?" I asked. "Why?"

"Because it's the only possibility left. I think we need to sit him down and confront him."

The next day we did exactly that, but Richie vehemently denied knowing anything about Dad's watch.

We let the incident pass, but several months later I was walking past the tall weeds behind my old, crumbling rabbit hutches when I noticed something glinting on a weed stalk. I walked over and saw a gold wheel wedged on a dried leaf. Then I saw a larger wheel on a stem nearby, and as I searched, I found many more pieces of my father's watch strewn in an arc, as if someone had flung them there.

This time when we confronted Richie, he confessed.

However, though he could be devious at times, Richie was making progress and toward the end of my college days had shown considerable spiritual interest.

Royal was still significantly delayed. In the early days he would rock back and forth on his bed, banging his head against the headboard, and he always had a hard time catching on to anything. Yet Mom steadily kept him moving forward. Anxious to please, a wonderful grin lighting up his face, Royal was huggable and helpful. My mother was raising both these boys with the same firm hand and unshakable love she had given Johnny and me.

chapter four

The decade of the sixties started as I turned twenty. What timing! I was to serve the majority of those years as editor of *Campus Life* magazine, near Chicago. Issues exploded on all Americans in ways that demanded response: Vietnam, drugs, sex, the Beatles, the civil rights movement, the assassinations of John F. Kennedy, Robert F. Kennedy, and Martin Luther King Jr.

The sexual revolution demanded frank coverage. We critiqued the "Playboy philosophy," but we also published a candid discussion of masturbation in order to help our teenage readers. The article was too candid for many adults, who angrily canceled subscriptions.

The Vietnam War grew larger and larger for all of us. We interviewed a Christian nineteen-year-old who was in the heart of the fighting; the photo that came in with the interview showed him standing in battle gear, looking like a bright student somehow displaced from his campus. We put the photo on the magazine's cover. Before the next issue was ready, we received word that he had been killed.

One week he was the cover story, the next a brief announcement that he was dead. Nineteen. Just like my aunt's brother. Like me on the navy ship. Why him but not me?

Racism continued to sear America, and the civil rights movement kept building momentum. I read Alan Paton's classic *Cry the Beloved Country,* and its thoroughly Christian perspective on the racial issues of South Africa simply blew me away. We made it *Campus Life's* book of the year, even though it had first been published more than a dozen years before.

As we learned more about what black people had to endure, we ran forums, interviews, biblical analysis. We had much to learn, and editors had to tread lightly to connect with skeptical white readers. For instance, my introduction to an article about the savage beating by Mississippi police of a black pastor, John Perkins, shows how thoroughly readers were unaware of the injustices suffered by blacks. The article was titled "I Wouldn't Expect Humans to Believe This . . ." My introduction warned that some would say, "Oh, that's exaggerated. Maybe a hundred years ago beatings of innocent blacks happened, but not today!" I knew it was vital that the author, Will Norton Jr., establish that Perkins was a Bible-believing preacher who had many young people go on to Christian colleges and into organizations like Campus Crusade, InterVarsity, and Youth for Christ.

Despite the fact that Perkins was innocent of wrongdoing, he had been beaten nearly to death, his blood all over the jail floor. Later, photos would show his eyes nearly swollen shut and bruises all over his head. A week later a doctor had to draw nearly a cup of fluid from a large knot on his head.

Perkins said then that he didn't tell many people about the experience because he didn't expect them to believe it. "You see," he said, "most white Christians don't want to believe this. They close their eyes to it. . . . They figure a black guy who gets in trouble isn't obeying the law. And the press plays up this protest thing so much that it sounds like some more people just trying to get away with something."

We ran the story not just to show the brutality being endured by black Christians but to show Perkins' attitude. "If the black man had the advantage," Perkins said, "he'd be just as bad, just as bad. So I can't hate the white man. It's a spiritual problem—black or white, we all need to be born again."

Some of us had been born again, but we were slow learners when it came to understanding how racism thrived through silence, ignorance, and bad theology.

Bad theology like the curse of Ham. Although one now hears little of that biblical interpretation, in the sixties it was held by a surprisingly large number of sincere, pious, and, yes, intelligent Christians. The Bible records a curse against Ham, one of Noah's sons. A convenient interpretation for slave owners was that blacks were the descendants of Ham and that the curse they were living with was simply God's judgment on them.

We ran a refutation of that theory in *Campus Life*. Hot correspondence ensued. Who were we to sit in judgment of faithful biblical teachers?

Our attempts to speak out did encourage some African-American readers. "Black is beautiful" was a sixties slogan we could heartily endorse. We published original oil paintings depicting beautiful African-Americans. A black youth leader said to the artist, "You're finally seeing our people!"

During that period, eloquent black evangelist Bill Pannell joined the headquarters staff of Youth for Christ—which published *Campus Life*—and tore veils of ignorance from our eyes. Sam Wolgemuth, YFC's president, wept at the revelations.

One evening in a youth meeting, I was listening to black evangelist Tom Skinner respond to questions about racial issues. Tom grabbed my attention with this statement: "Moses married a nigger, and when his sister, Miriam, complained, he struck her with leprosy!"

What had Tom said? I couldn't believe the force of the assertion and his use of the word *nigger*. Of course, as a black he could use it as he wished, but this was long before white ears had heard anyone use the word in a church. In today's talk-show environment nothing shocks, but then his words jolted us. This was a time of visceral rejection of interracial marriage. The idea that Moses, of all patriarchs, had married a black woman was startling enough. Even more sobering was God's judgment of leprosy. Had the real reason why God struck down Miriam been her complaining about her brother marrying a black?

I've since talked with knowledgeable theologians about this, and certainly it is probable that Moses' wife, Zipporah, had very dark skin.

And racism as the cause of God's fury against Miriam is at the very least more credible than the curse of Ham application. But regardless of the merits of Tom's statement, it made me think about the whole issue of interracial marriage and the hypocrisies sustaining miscegenation laws. How bitter that a white man could force himself on a slave woman and father a child—his child!—and reject the baby as his own son or daughter. How ironic that one drop of black blood supposedly made such children inferior, yet it had been the promiscuous whites who had sired them.

"Moses married a nigger." The statement shouted at me. Some months after hearing it, I was in a restaurant with a publisher who asked what my next book was going to be. I said immediately, "I think I should write a book titled *Moses Married a Nigger.*" I told him I'd write about our intense reactions to interracial marriage. The book would speak to Christian complicity in the plight of blacks in America, of how we were often oblivious to our own prejudice.

His eyes did not light up at the idea.

I regret I never wrote that book, as well as another I had outlined—a fantasy novel. It would have depicted a reversal of black inferiority mythology. An American crew of black and white astronauts would escape a disintegrating earth by blasting off into space. They would successfully establish a New America on a distant world and after a few hundred years have a society much like the United States, with one exception: blacks would become dominant. And they would develop a mythology explaining the "obvious" inferiority of whites. They wouldn't need a biblical curse of Ham; they would use Hitler and slavery to build their case.

In my fictional New America, instructors would teach "obvious" lessons: black is rich and full of life and meaning; white is washed out and ugly. "Simply look about," they would teach, "at the repulsiveness of squirming white grubs, of maggots in the putrid white flesh of a cadaver." Naturally, I would have a lovely black woman in this novel fall in love with a young white man, and everyone would be amazed that she could sink that low.

~

I was being stretched in every direction, working day and night and loving every minute of it. I had little time to think of romance. When I was asked to direct a YFC program in nearby Wisconsin in my "spare time," I had no idea I'd meet my life mate there. In fact, when I first met Jeanette Austin, there was no blip on either of our screens. She was a high school club kid, strictly off-limits for a YFC staffer, and she was in love with a college student. Since her dad was chair of the local YFC board, I would stay at their dairy farm.

One Saturday I sat at her dining room table with plans for the evening's rally spread out. Concentrating on the program, I barely heard a little boy come up and ask me something. "Not now," I said, shooing him away.

Jeanette in the kitchen observed this and thought, *This guy doesn't like kids; so much for him!*

After the rally that evening, my car filled up with teenagers. One by one I dropped them off at their homes until only Jeanette was still in the backseat. I turned around and said, "I'd invite you up here to the front, but you know how it is with appearances."

Unknown to me, my statement stunned her. She had no idea why I would say such a crazy thing. She rode out to the farm wondering what sort of cold fish I was. The next day her telephone hummed as she spread the word to her girlfriends about my strange aloofness. Not only did I have no time for little kids but, incredibly, I wouldn't even let her sit in the front seat.

Of course, I was simply exercising caution. Years before in Pennsylvania, my YFC director learned I had met a high school girl at the office one Saturday morning. "Was anyone else there?" he demanded. "Don't you realize she could say anything about what happened?" I had never seen him so intense. "It doesn't matter if the girl is an innocent, wonderful kid. You just don't take that chance!"

My resulting caution made me seem like a prude to Jeanette. Yet I was oblivious to that as we worked together on club and rally activities.

By the time she graduated from high school and came to Chicago to train as an RN, we had become good friends.

Then more than friends. Her earlier romance long over, we started dating and found we thought alike on most things—including, to her surprise, the subject of kids. She was full of energy and enthusiasm, with lots of spunk, climbing aboard busses to anywhere in Chicago and rising to whatever emergency might occur.

"You remind me of Shirley Temple," I told her. "In one of her movies, an adult warns her she can't do something. She stands up straight and tall and declares, 'I'm very self-reliant, you know!'"

Over the years that phrase became a byword between us. She would take on a tough challenge, and we would agree that she was, as usual, very self-reliant.

Also, fellow nurses and patients alike called her "Little Miss Sunshine." A candid shot from our wedding captures that quality and Jeanette's *joie de vivre*. It was taken an instant before she was to start down the aisle toward me. The joy and intensity on her face said she was ready to live life fully with her new husband.

One Saturday after we had been married, Jeanette and I and two other couples took in some of Chicago's sights: the famed aquarium full of exotic, colorful creatures; the planetarium next door with its dramatic star shows; sailboats on Lake Michigan's blue waters. By late afternoon we were in our car, ready to go home.

As we waited for the light at an expressway ramp, I was settled in the backseat, my eyes scanning the people on the sidewalks. Close by the car were several groups of black people. One woman turned her head, then locked onto my watching eyes. She seemed intent on staring at me. As the wind blew at her dark, shabby clothes, she shifted her body but did not shift her gaze from me. Her eyes seemed to be probing, studying, evaluating.

I was taken aback. Did she wonder why I was looking? Did she resent me? Did she resent all of us in this car, with our privileges and opportunities? For long seconds we kept staring, each of us alien to the other. I was about to escape this dreary part of Chicago. She was trapped in it.

Or was she? Maybe she was content. Yet my gut said she knew plenty of poverty and trouble. Why was she staring at me second after long second? Could we talk? Might I help her—or she me?

The green light and car's acceleration broke our gaze. As we shot forward, I turned my head back but she had moved. Speeding toward our home in Wheaton, I barely heard the conversations around me. I felt a sense of loss, that somehow I should have talked with this woman, reached out to her, shared with her, learned what was in her eyes.

chapter five

More than once I thought about the gaze of the black woman in Chicago. But Jeanette, now an RN, didn't dwell on images and theory. She amazed me in many ways, among them her practical attitude of "Don't sit there; do it!" When she heard that volunteers for Head Start were needed in Chicago's south side, she signed on. I worried about my young wife on her day off parking her car and taking risks in a notoriously dangerous area, but she was determined—particularly if it meant helping children.

Like me, Jeanette had been influenced by her parents' example. For instance, when she was little, her parents would often bring into their home for weekends Cora Mae, a lonely, obese teenager from the Wisconsin School for the Visually Handicapped. "She was fun," Jeanette remembers. "Cora Mae's one eye looked bad, and the other eye had been removed, so she had a glass eye. She loved to take it out, show us her empty eye socket, and give us little kids the creeps. My mom laughed a lot with her, running to the mailbox on bare feet over our long gravel driveway with this chubby, half-blind teenager."

Jeanette was like her mom. She would reach out to children with a ready laugh and a spirit of love and optimism. In the sixties conflagration she dwelt on bringing hope. She found it hard to understand why I felt so weighed down by terrible events in the world.

One afternoon early in our marriage we were enjoying a beach, walking over grass nearly smothered by sand. Our fingers touched but I was distracted. The blades of grass under the heavy sand reminded me of a little boy named Jeffrey.

The papers had reported a tragic story. Jeffrey had polished his stepdad's shoes and dropped one out a window and—as five-year-olds do—had spilled a can of paint. His stepdad had beaten him with a belt for days. He'd tied him to a doorknob so he couldn't sit. Finally he'd beaten him to death.

Despite our romantic walk, this story came out of my mouth, breaking the mood. "And after it had happened," I said, "Jeffrey's mother told police that when his stepfather threatened to kill him, the little boy just said, 'Daddy, I love you.'"

We sat on some rocks, looking at waves as I asked, "How can God make such a world?"

"It saddens me," Jeanette said. "If the boy were next door, I'd rescue him. But I can't dwell on it. I can't allow it to make me miserable."

But I could and did. If I were shaping my life serving a God of love, how did I reconcile his allowing all these children to be battered by words and blunt objects? Were we mere molecules and dirt? Rabbits? Or made in God's image—eternal, moral beings?

Somehow this all came into sharpest relief when evil was done to children. After all, it was Jesus who said it would be better that a millstone were tied around a person's neck and he be thrown into the sea than that he should offend a little one.

My parents back home in the Poconos had been raising Richie and Royal for seven years now and had added their sister Margie to the family. Royal was learning basic skills. Richie made faith commitments. Margie was looking forward to growing up and becoming a nurse, so we offered to bring her to Chicago for schooling.

But then my mother received a call from her caseworker. The children were to be returned to their mother. We were saddened at the news, for we feared for them.

A few years went by. Then we heard that Richie, now seventeen, was getting into trouble. One evening my mother called me with the worst news of all. Our good friend and next-door neighbor, Mrs. Prosser, had been murdered. Someone had killed her with a shotgun.

"The police think Richie may have done it," Mother said on the phone. "They think he's been hanging around here. They're hunting for him." She paused. "But it's not sure." Her tone carried just a trace of hope, but we both knew the likely truth.

How could this be? Mother had felt led to reach out to these children, to nurture them in the love of Christ. They were responding. How could they be pulled away into disruption, temptation, devastation?

I took a long, long walk on a prairie path after that phone call. I moved briskly, my body working pleasurably but my mind in turmoil. Suddenly I burst out with my complaint against God. "How could you do this?" I demanded. "Just when Richie was responding, he gets pulled out of our home. And then Mrs. Prosser gets murdered!"

I stopped at a dried-out pond that I had stood beside a few weeks before when it had been full of algae and suffocating fish. I'd watched the little fish sticking their mouths out of the dying pond, desperate for oxygen. Now it was all dried muck, the fish dead. "Your world is beautiful—but brutal," I accused. "Wasn't Richie just like those fish? Trapped, doomed. Richie the victim who goes on to victimize. Lord, how can you run your world with such capricious horror?"

Never before had I prayed like that. I prayed a very long time with many tears.

The response was crystal clear: "I'm not upset by your prayers." On the contrary, it was as if God had been waiting for me to look evil full in the face and confront him.

God seemed to say, "How do you think I feel about Richie? About Mrs. Prosser? Haven't I wept over them? Haven't I sent my Son to die for them?"

This flowed into me as a personal, forceful connection with God. I sensed that he was drawing me into his perspective, that he was calling me almost as a colleague to join forces in extending his love, to intercede for others in their helplessness—and that he was indeed in charge, transcending all tragedies.

It turned out that Richie had committed the murder. Unknown to my parents, he had been staying in my grandfather's abandoned trailer and had decided he needed a car. He went next door, tried to take Mrs. Prosser's sedan, but she confronted him. She told him she was going to call the police.

Unfortunately, he had a shotgun, and in his panic he shot her in the face. Then he fled and disappeared; she died on the driveway.

Eventually Richie was apprehended in Florida. He was convicted and is now serving a life sentence.

Years ago Jeanette and I took our three birth children to visit Richie. As we drove up the long hill to the prison in Dallas, Pennsylvania, I said to them, "How would you like to have been Richie, as a teenager riding shackled up this hill to a place from which he would never return?" Yet over the years, through my parents and other Christians, he has found God. When he entered prison, he could barely write a legible letter; now he communicates like a college grad. Through the Jaycees he has found opportunities for sports, education, and enterprise. During his decades in prison he has become an articulate, thoughtful person.

The troubles of such children are not issues of race but issues of the heart and spirit. Whenever I'm tempted to think of the dysfunction in urban communities as a black problem, I have only to think of Richie and all the institutional and personal failures which contributed so greatly to the tragedy.

But the sixties were not all chaos and confrontation. Jeanette and I experienced a lot of joy, and the world was full of new music and great hopes and even walking on the moon. In fact, the first men stepped onto the moon the day our first child was born, a birth which affected me far beyond my expectations.

My ideal for having children would have been instant five-year-olds. Anything to avoid the diapers, squalling, food-smeared high chairs, and general chaos. But Jeanette early in our marriage began preparing me. "Aren't pregnant women beautiful?" she asked one day.

I scrunched up my eyebrows. "What?"

She picked up a magazine and found several ads featuring pregnant models in elegant maternity clothes.

"Look at her—isn't she beautiful?"

Of course I said yes, but this was all new thinking for me. And when Jeanette did become pregnant, she embraced the adventure of it in a way that amazed me. Nausea and discomforts were mere annoyances; no one appreciated being pregnant more than Jeanette nor anticipated birth with more elemental joy.

But those were my wife's feelings. This was her drama. I was still concentrating on "the main event," my work challenges that seemed larger than my capacities.

One moment totally changed all that. Jeanette had calmly said before dawn one morning that her contractions were starting. We raced to the hospital, Jeanette still as calm as I was anxious.

A few hours later as I was pacing in the "father's room," I was called to the door. I could see Jeanette being wheeled down the hall, smiling at me like Miss America. The nurse was holding a baby in her arms and stopped in front of me. "You have a girl, Mr. Myra."

She turned the little bundle so I could see her better. Then came the most surprising instant of my life. The moment my eyes met those of my newborn child, all those ideas of instant five-year-olds were swallowed up. My little girl was looking right at me! Wide-open, bright-blue eyes startled me with her awareness, drinking me in. I was stunned by her. Michelle, my daughter, was already a full participant in her new world, mere minutes old but fully alive.

I have never recovered from that moment, nor do I ever want to. I was so blown away by the experience that I wrote a little book about it.

A few years later came the drama of a breech birth. This time it was the early seventies, and fathers were expected to be in the delivery room. I wasn't at all sure I liked the idea, and I wondered later if the doctors might have been just as glad if I'd stayed out.

The instant the birth actually began, one of them reached way into the birth canal, grabbed the baby by the shoulder, and pulled him with strong force and near-panicky speed. The urgency of it all startled me. I thought of the movie *Hawaii*, in which the missionary successfully delivered a breech baby, to the astonishment of the islanders, who always let them die. Obviously, you had to move fast so the baby would not be deprived of oxygen.

In what seemed to me record time they delivered a boy.

The birth of our son, Todd, meant we now had a healthy girl and boy, and both Jeanette and I figured our family was complete. I had come from a family with two children, Jeanette a family with three. Two seemed a very good number to me.

But a few years after Todd's birth Jeanette got a call from a woman in our church. Five neglected children in one family needed homes. Four other church families had agreed to take one child each. The idea was that if the children were all placed in families from one church, they could see each other on Sundays, and other connections could be arranged. Would we be willing to become the fifth family and take the seventeen-month-old?

Jeanette, with a sparkle in her eye, asked me what I thought. I had lots of questions. How long might this be for? How complicated might this get? I was hesitant, but the children's needs seemed compelling, so I agreed.

But the event never happened. The family fled the state.

This experience encouraged thoughts about enlarging our family. Clearly we could care for another child. I loved Michelle and Todd and felt tremendous fulfillment being their dad. And I thought, *If the house were to start burning down, what would I rush to save? My unfinished manuscripts and books? Photos? No, Todd and Michelle. And if they are that precious, perhaps one more might add to our joy.*

Certainly Jeanette loved hearing me say that. So we began planning to have another child.

chapter six

*I*n February 1975 Jeanette and I flew to San Diego for YFC's annual midwinter convention. We'd attended many of these together and had loved every one of them, but this was to be our last.

We had more than one reason for feelings of loss. Not long after deciding we wanted a third child, Jeanette had gotten blissfully pregnant. But then one evening in the summer, when I came home from the office, she told me she had suffered a miscarriage. Now she was dealing with uncertainty and dashed hopes. So far she had not been able to get pregnant again. Should we adjust our intentions to have a third child, especially considering my recent decision to leave YFC?

We'd never anticipated leaving. We had met in YFC, had our first date in YFC. It had bonded us in mutual ministry. Twenty years before, YFC had ignited my spiritual passion and ever since had stretched me, challenged me, and driven me to my knees. This dynamic movement that had spun off dozens of evangelical organizations had shaped my formative years and put into me a determination to do all God asked.

I had read during college, "A man with a burning purpose draws others to himself, who help him to fulfill it." For years that statement had riveted my attention—and that was what had happened. Marvelous men and women of extraordinary talent had joined me as *Campus Life* grew from a house organ with a circulation of thirty thousand to a broader magazine with a hundred and fifty thousand readers. Philip Yancey came on staff and he kept amazing me; every time I gave him a promotion, he was ready for more, and soon he had taken over most of my job.

Which was wonderful, and the entire publishing team was bonded together. But because YFC hit a financial wall, we couldn't move forward with the growth that would have kept me challenged.

The San Diego convention therefore was bittersweet. After the meetings were over, Jeanette and I drove up the California coast, feeling separated from shared roots.

We stayed for a couple of days in Carmel. We walked the beach at sunset and enjoyed a little cabin with a fireplace. As we left Carmel and headed for San Francisco, we wondered what was next. Would we have another child? What work would I do?

I still had plenty of burning passion for the future. I was talking to Paul Robbins, also a YFC vice president in transition, about starting a new publishing ministry. I had lots of books I wanted to write.

Yet with all the possibilities, I kept remembering the phrase I sang often in college days: "For who am I, that I should choose my way?" I was determined to seek God's plans.

A few months later I stepped off a plane in Pittsburgh and scanned the terminal for Duncan Brown, a businessman on the executive committee of Christianity Today, Inc. (CTI). I spied him in dapper clothes, striding energetically toward me. His handshake was firm and his smile gregarious. Soon we were in a restaurant talking about my experience with magazines and Christianity Today's needs for publishing expertise.

For months Fred Smith had been talking to me on the phone about CT's problems. Fred too was a businessman on CT's board; it had been right here in Pittsburgh that I'd first heard Fred speak at a previous YFC convention. His earthy wisdom and humor had taken all of us by storm. Fred later became chairman of YFC, and we had become friends. Now each time he called, he'd ask, "Who could go into CT and solve the problems there?" Finally, after I had repeatedly failed to suggest a viable name, he'd said, "I think you're the man."

So here I was talking to Duncan. After discussing CT's challenges, we were soon back in his sporty Cadillac convertible for the return ride to the airport. As he waved good-bye and drove off, I was impressed by his humble spirit. Duncan had chaired Billy Graham's Pittsburgh crusade and was a tireless worker for the Salvation Army. It struck me as I headed for the Chicago gate: *This guy doesn't need to do this. He's young, handsome, and wealthy. He could be out there spending his chips instead of giving himself for God's causes.*

My sense was that Fred and Duncan were people I could highly respect. Perhaps the future was becoming clear after all.

One morning in early June my alarm jangled in my ear at 5:30. Jumping upright, I realized the day would be decisive for my career, for I was to meet with CT's executive committee. After scrambling into my business suit and eating a fast bowl of cereal, I kissed Jeanette and tossed my briefcase and hang-up bag into my old Pontiac.

At Chicago's O'Hare Airport I pulled up to the tollbooth, opened the window, and tossed in the change. When the sign went green, I hit the gas.

Nothing happened. The engine was dead.

I turned the key. Nothing, not even a groan.

This was crazy. This had never happened to me before. How could it possibly happen here, on this of all days, in a tollbooth with cars behind me and a plane I had to catch?

Yes, I had to catch the 7:00 flight to D.C.! It was 6:30. CTI's executive committee would be meeting at 10:00 in the Washington Building, its members having come from Dallas, Boston, Minneapolis, Nashville, and Pittsburgh—and the agenda was me.

It didn't help that it was already 7:30 in Washington. I turned the key and racked my brain as to how to get the car moving. Finally, in desperation I got out, put my shoulder to it, and pushed the car off the roadway.

Grabbing my luggage, I hailed a man pulling out of a tollbooth, and he kindly picked me up. I wondered what sort of exorbitant parking ticket I might get for leaving my car there, but at least I was moving toward the terminal. Once there I called Jeanette, told her about the car, and heard her say with her usual confidence, "Somehow we'll take care of it."

So I made my flight and after a cab ride from National Airport was ushered into CT's conference room. Fred and Duncan were there. So was Harold Ockenga, chair of CT's board, and Maxey Jarman, chair of the committee. Harold, a primary founder of modern American evangelicalism, had been first president of the National Association of Evangelicals and first president of Fuller Seminary in Pasadena while pastoring historic Park Street Church in Boston. Quite a feat! Maxey was the Jarman of Jarman Shoes who had built the giant Genesco Corporation. Also present was Clayton Bell, pastor of Highland Park Presbyterian in Dallas and son of L. Nelson Bell, who with Billy Graham had founded the magazine.

We discussed the problems. CT had expanded into book clubs, book publishing, and other enterprises, then suddenly was awash in red ink; circulation had dipped dramatically.

They asked me to step out of the room. When I was called back, I was handed a job description with the titles president, publisher, and chief executive officer.

Was this really happening? It seemed extraordinary that these giants of the Christian world were handing CT over to me at age thirty-five.

"Is the job description satisfactory?" Maxey asked.

"Looks good to me," I said.

Then we discussed my plan to commute for an extended time instead of moving to Washington. This seemed only logical to me. I was still making the transition out of *Campus Life*, and the situation at CT seemed precarious. This was during Watergate, and many board members, fed up with "the mess in Washington," wanted CT to move to Dallas or Atlanta or Chicago and get a fresh start. If I moved, perhaps I'd soon have to move again.

Also, joyously, Jeanette was again pregnant. What if, after all the effort of moving to Washington, CT folded?

But Maxey was uneasy about my commuting and said so. However, Duncan pulled him aside, and I could hear him saying quietly, "He knows CT may not make it."

They conferred a little more, and then Maxey turned to me and asked, "When can you start?"

"Right now," I said. "I have everything with me."

That night at the Washington Hotel, having put in a whirlwind day, I phoned Jeanette, then lay down for a sound night's sleep. But something strange and unprecedented happened. Always, no matter how much is on my mind, I eventually fall asleep—except that night. My mind was on green alert, churning on the events of the day. How was it possible that this prestigious group had just handed me the *New York Times* of evangelicalism?

I kept trying to shut down my brain, but it insisted on exploring ideas and strategies. I felt I had just been handed the keys to unlimited potential in just the field which most energized me.

Finally, with dawn's light and no sleep at all, I got up, had breakfast, and plunged into my first day's urgencies.

The CT offices were on the top floor of the Washington Building, overlooking the White House. At that time of Watergate, as now, Washington represented both dark tragedy and grand potential. Over the next months, CT's strong national influence weighed on me as with colleagues I would sketch out financial plans and at night would walk by the Washington and Lincoln Memorials, praying for wisdom and planning for board meetings.

The trajectory that had started in the Poconos and continued in Wheaton seemed not my doing but God's layering challenge after challenge on me. Mostly I just felt amazed. I thought often of the promise from Jeremiah, "Call unto me, and I will answer thee, and show thee great and mighty things" (Jer. 33:3 KJV). Yet I was sobered by Jeremiah's blunt counsel, "Seekest thou great things for thyself? Seek them not" (Jer. 45:5 KJV).

For years I had been saying to friends, "If I had tried to predict in the Poconos what great and mighty things might happen—if I had created fantastical scenarios of space travel or international exploits—I couldn't have imagined what God actually did."

Yet publishing was just part of that. Equally spectacular to me was marriage and birth. The miracle of children and all their potential was great and mighty in the same sense of God doing his work of creation with us and through us. What could be more profound than loving a new, eternal person and participating in his or her growth and unlimited possibilities?

~

On the second day of November I was anxious to get home from Washington, for we hoped to soon experience the birth of our third child. I finished at the CT offices and hopped a cab, riding past the Smithsonian buildings and over the bridge to National Airport.

Lugging briefcase and hang-up bag toward the United Airlines counter, I smiled at the memory of my recent conversation at Wheaton Travel. "I'm tired of flying American," I had said to the agent. "Week after week after week, all they serve for breakfast is little red hot dogs."

The woman laughed.

"I like the hot dogs. But . . ."

She grinned and started writing the new ticket. "We'll put you on United this week." Later on the phone she told me her colleagues kept laughing about my "little red hot dogs."

As I entered United's plane and settled into my seat for the umpteenth ride home to Illinois, I sagged back. The pace in Washington was flat out, but the commuting had gone surprisingly well. Never once on all those flights during what would eventually become nine months of commuting did I get seriously delayed. Jeanette, instead of being stressed by it, actually enjoyed the routine. I was gone three days but only two nights, and while I was away she'd scurry to get things done. Sometimes when I returned at a remarkably consistent 6:45 P.M. on Thursdays, she was sitting on the porch beside little Michelle and Todd, waiting for me.

That's what I was hoping for as I drove from O'Hare and finally rounded the corner of our street—I'd begun to love that new family tradition. But as I pulled in the drive, the porch was empty.

I wasn't surprised. Surely Jeanette was concentrating on all kinds of preparations. Nothing enthused her more than birth, and since the doctors had decided to induce her, she knew roughly when it was all to begin. Although no one was on the porch that evening, inside I found an excited little family.

Two days later it was a blustery, snowy day as we drove to the doctor's office, then directly to the hospital. I sat beside Jeanette as a nurse started an IV which would get the contractions going, and I was surprised at how quickly they began. Soon we were in the delivery room, and in contrast to Todd's more dramatic birth, this one proceeded like clockwork. Would it be a boy or girl? We didn't care. We only knew we felt much joy when Gregory was born and completed our little family.

A few months later Jeanette and I were in Virginia house hunting, with tiny Greg in a basket. The CT board was vacillating on moving or staying put, but we decided I'd commuted long enough. The organization was doing well enough for me to take the risk.

So with our realtor we inspected house after house just outside the beltway. Actually, it was kind of fun having Greg along. We'd pull into a driveway, put Greg just inside the front door in his little basket, and do a quick tour. Then out to the car and on to the next one. We did about twenty-five houses that way, and despite the jostling Greg stayed perfectly peaceful.

We found a house in, of all places, a subdivision named Camelot. And Camelot it seemed to us, its cherry tree–lined streets and woodsy setting in close range of the beltway.

In a Florida hotel room, as I was getting ready to meet with CT's full board for the first time, the past year's events suddenly struck me as humorous. In a few minutes I would report that we had finished the year three hundred thousand dollars to the good. This was because the magazine had been underpriced, so we had roughly doubled the price and offered an advance subscription. That was the extent of my genius.

As I looked in the mirror and adjusted my tie, laughter bubbled up. Here I was the kid from the Poconos, and I'd soon be greeted by all those older movers and shakers and academics as the whiz kid of the moment. How crazy life was.

British author Rosemary Budd speaks to this humor, saying that our journey with God is into humility and the truth about ourselves—and that "the music of humility is laughter."

The music of humility is laughter. What a freeing reality! A small publishing decision had enabled CT to regain its momentum. Publishing mountains yet to climb were huge, but I had a settled sense that it was more than I who was directing things and that I was—to use the title of Ken Taylor's autobiography—on some sort of "Guided Tour."

In March our family set out from Illinois to our new home in Virginia. The moving van was far behind us. At 11:00 P.M. we arrived at a motel outside the capital.

The kids were asleep in the car, so Jeanette and I carried them inside and put them into the beds. "Nothing more beautiful than a child asleep," I said as I stared in the semidarkness at the barely visible faces of Michelle, Todd, and baby Greg.

"They're so innocent now," Jeanette said, an obvious reference to shenanigans in the car. "But I love them to pieces." She bent over and kissed each one, then started getting ready for bed.

"Jeanette, mind if I go out for coffee?" I asked.

She cocked her head dubiously. My patient wife was used to my writing very late at night. "Really?" she asked. "It's been a long drive." However, she also knew I'd slept a little during the time she drove. She shrugged at me with a smile and waved me off.

"I won't be long," I said as I slipped out the door.

Actually, I was pumped with all sorts of ideas I wanted to work on. During the long ride I'd been thinking about not only CT publishing but concepts for books, including one about Santa Claus. I drove up Route 50, turned on Little River Turnpike, and found the wonderful donut shop close to Camelot.

What could be better? Not yet midnight and here I was with good coffee, a chocolate-frosted donut, a long yellow pad, and ideas to work on. The state of Virginia was agreeing with me!

For some time I'd thought about Christian parents not knowing what to say about Santa Claus. Yet Saint Nicholas had been a remarkable Christian. Why not talk about his having been real, how he loved Jesus, and how Santa Claus reminds us we should, too?

The idea had been there for some time, but now the words came flowing to the rhythm of "'Twas the Night before Christmas." Todd, Michelle, and Greg—actually all our family—were becoming the characters.

I closed the pad around 1:30, and as I drove back to the motel wondered about my drivenness to keep writing. Ever since I was in first grade, I had to be writing something. Once when I'd read a comment by C. S. Lewis to the effect that the bird must sing and the lion roar, it resonated inside. I simply had to write. Yet my primary work was publishing. That included editing, which I loved, but also advertising, circulation, accounting, administration, and overall leadership.

Three strong forces, then, weighed on me even as they energized me: family, publishing, and writing. Balancing them was a constant challenge, and the pressures would grow stronger in the future.

chapter seven

My cousin Dave Christensen had been best man at my wedding. As a young doctor, he had gone as a missionary to Africa, where he'd fallen in love with a Swiss nurse named Elsbeth. However, Elsbeth had wanted nothing to do with him, at least romantically. David was determined to win her. After their wedding, the two of them would tell stories of their courtship, eyes dancing with the humor, romance, and African lore. It was all so compelling, I decided to write it up as a book.

But before I could get started, everything changed. Jeanette and I and the kids were visiting Dave and his little family at my parents' home in the Poconos. Elsbeth was not her usual self. As we walked past the lake, Dave told me Elsbeth was getting out of breath climbing stairs. "It could be serious," he said.

A few days later when we were back home, Dave called to say it was serious indeed. Elsbeth had acute leukemia; she was not expected to live.

Months later after extensive treatment Elsbeth was in remission. Jeanette and I visited with her and Dave, driving out to the magnificent Longwood Gardens near Philadelphia. As we walked the grounds, we found it hard to enjoy the striking colors and shapes of the orchids, cacti, and palms, in light of Elsbeth's prognosis.

That evening we all went to a restaurant and talked about their hopes and fears, about their two little boys, Eric and Davey. We talked about their courtship experiences in Africa, all of us reaching for the laughter and the good times of the years just behind them.

And we talked about their adopted daughter, Karba.

Elsbeth had first met Karba in a tiny Nigerian village. Karba was two years old, and her belly was distended from worms and poor nutrition; her arms were like sticks. Karba was an eighth child. Among hill tribes, the eighth child was taboo that brought disaster. One tribe drowned such babies; another sold each eighth child into slavery. Karba's tribe would dispose of an eighth child by simply putting it out on the rocks to die.

Newborn Karba had been left on the rocks. A Christian chief named Musa had chanced upon her and had brought her back to live with his family. However, even though Musa tried to protect her, Karba's survival was far from assured. When something was stolen, she would be blamed and beaten for it. She was malnourished and constantly ill.

Early in their marriage David and Elsbeth brought Karba into their little family. And now in Philadelphia they had tales of this little bush child transformed. Karba confidently got good grades and among other things could carry the entire class's tray of milk cartons on her head—much to the amazement of her third-grade classmates.

Elsbeth was full of humor that evening, laughing, telling stories. Yet the shadows haunted her. As we finished the meal, she told us about a dream she'd had the night before: "I was on a boat and black people were clinging to the sides," Elsbeth said. "A white man kept stamping on their hands, forcing them into the water to their deaths. I went to others on the boat, pointing the man out, saying, 'Look what he's doing. He's already killed people.' Then someone told me, 'He's after you because you're telling on him.'

"I then saw him at a window aiming a gun at me. I was terrified and called for the police, who arrested him. Then the police let him go! He was at the window again, aiming at me again!"

After the dinner and during the next months, I recorded many hours of interviews with David and Elsbeth about Africa and about the final chapters of her life.

During her remission she was able to participate in a wedding, and as she walked down the aisle, soft lights from the candles diffused into sparkling beads. To her, the light from the candles was a lovely invitation, beckoning her forward to life, to light, to a warm welcome.

She thought, *Karba and David are here, but they can't walk with me, can't be absorbed into the light with me.*

Elsbeth told me that this was her vision of how she thought it would be at her funeral. Although David and Karba would be there, she'd be walking into the welcoming light alone. Elsbeth said that this was the way she wanted the book to end: "Here are all the people in front of the casket, mourning. They don't see me walking into the light, the door to heaven. If they could only see how beautiful it is."

Living through the experiences with them made me face once again the deepest questions. It also intrigued me that Elsbeth had been so transformed in her relationship with black people. Years before, when as a young nurse she had arrived in Nigeria from Switzerland, she had been startled and apprehensive to see only black people everywhere. But after years of ministering with all sorts of Africans, she built deep friendships. When her missionary term was up, she hated the thought of leaving her beloved Africans.

When at the start of her leukemia she had been brought in crisis to Philadelphia's Temple University Hospital, she saw all the black faces of the personnel. Though the hospital was in a "dangerous" area, she felt wonderfully safe and at home because all the faces around her were like the faces she loved in Nigeria.

Elsbeth eventually died, and at her funeral I thought about her description of how she was entering the light.

Two years after I joined CT, the board decided to relocate the organization near Chicago, where it could get that fresh start. Jeanette and I moved our family back to Illinois.

It worked out well. Paul Robbins joined us and became chief operating officer. We stabilized *Christianity Today* and launched *Leadership,* a journal for pastors. *Campus Life* ran into publishing difficulties and we brought it into CTI, then later acquired *Today's Christian Woman.*

Jeanette happily did volunteer work at church and school. When Greg was in fourth grade, she helped out at a home for severely damaged children and provided respite care in our home for a profoundly handicapped boy named Brian. And hearing on the radio of the critical need for foster parents, she attended an orientation meeting of the Department of Children and Family Services for Illinois.

She told me when she got home, "The trainers, Jane and Diane, are foster mothers themselves. You'd like them. They really love these kids." She was persuading me to attend training sessions so our family could be licensed for her respite work. "It's only seven sessions," she said. "It'll be a good experience for you."

To support her ministry to children, I said yes.

An autumn rainstorm gusted against our umbrellas one evening as we hurried up the steps of DCFS headquarters. As we removed our coats, we saw four other couples talking and filling out forms. "That's Diane, with the black hair," Jeanette said, nodding toward an attractive, well-dressed woman in her forties. She then pointed out Jane, about the same age but more plainly dressed. Both were Master Foster Parents, well qualified since they'd been in the foster care trenches themselves.

Soon we were sitting in a circle with Jane, Diane, and the other couples. Under my fingers were forms to fill out: question after question about our marriage, birth children, parents, life stories, extended family attitudes. How would we discipline children? Where in our home would a child sleep? Although I liked Jane and Diane's leadership and passion for children, I wasn't thrilled that I had to fill out forms and do homework each week. Wasn't this Jeanette's outreach?

As we drove home to the baby-sitter and our (hopefully) sleeping kids, Jeanette said, "You can sure see why Diane and Jane give themselves to these children. So many are traumatized from terrible situations. You can hardly help but catch their vision."

I agreed. "They're very impressive women."

But neither Jeanette nor I identified with the way caring for kids had taken over their lives. They had ended up adopting and adding bedrooms to their homes and getting bigger cars to haul around larger families. They had become advocates in the schools for their adopted children and become totally immersed in the monumental challenges. I wondered what their husbands did for a living that allowed for such heavy family commitments. Not for a moment did we think this was something for us—we were there just to help out for a week or two at a time.

Six months later after being trained, getting fingerprinted, and having our home inspected, we were officially licensed. Late one afternoon Jeanette was starting supper when the phone rang. She wondered if it might be my cousin Dave, who was at a Chicago medical convention and was taking the train out for a visit. But it was DCFS with an emergency.

The social worker was calling from the police station. "We have a two-and-a-half-year-old who needs to be placed immediately." The doctor who had set the boy's broken leg some weeks before had been shocked when it was the parents who brought him back in to get the cast off. The unemployed father had at least once beaten the mother; the couple did not live together. For many reasons the doctor was convinced that the father had caused the break by throwing the boy against a wall, and he was upset that the father still had the boy.

DCFS was called. Soon the family was at the police station, and when the boy was taken from the father, he exploded and began screaming at the police. The mother was hysterical, shouting, "Why now? Why are you taking him now?" As the social worker talked to Jeanette on the phone, she sounded stressed. She feared the parents would follow her as she left the station.

We were expecting Dave to arrive for dinner, but Jeanette told the caseworker she should bring the boy. When Dave called from the train station, I left to pick him up as Jeanette hastened to borrow a crib. When Dave and I returned, we started assembling it.

The bell rang. Our kids started down the stairs. When Jeanette opened the door, we saw the caseworker holding a little boy with blond, straight hair.

We all greeted him, trying not to scare him. The woman held his belongings in a small plastic bag that smelled strongly of cigarette smoke. "The doctor doesn't want him to walk until he sees him again in a week," she said.

Jeanette asked questions and Dave checked out Tim's leg. The phone rang; a police detective wanted to know if the child and case-worker were okay.

We agreed that I should take the boy to the family room, so I picked up the small-boned little guy and carried him. He was fair like Greg, with similar features. I longed to comfort him. "You doing okay, Tim?" I asked as I eased the sober little boy onto an overstuffed chair.

He nodded, looking at the fireplace, then started getting up from the chair. "Coat, please," he said. "Go home now."

"Not yet, little guy." I picked up some children's books and pointed out some pictures. But he was agitated and said again, "Coat. Go home now."

In the training sessions we had been asked how we would feel if suddenly we were taken from our family and put all alone in a foreign country. Tim had experienced rapid dislocation. Just hours earlier he had been riding with his parents to visit the doctor, but now he was trapped here with strangers.

"Tim, I'm sorry we can't get your coat and take you home right now," I said. "But you're going to be just fine here for a little while."

He turned his head, locked his eyes on mine, and started pleading fervently, "Home to Daddy. See Daddy. Pleeeease!" He drew out the word *please* as if by straining it for long seconds, he could somehow make a crazy world understand.

That night Tim ate little at dinner. However, when Jeanette rocked him quietly on her lap, soothing him, she was surprised at how easily he fell asleep.

Dave had remarried since Elsbeth's death and now had children from both marriages as well as Karba. We talked well past midnight but not a great deal about foster care. As father of a first-generation African-American child, he faced the unique challenges of raising her near Philadelphia. We, on the other hand, were not thinking of long-term commitments at all.

Next morning Tim cheerfully played on the carpet with our dog Sam and with Greg. When the children left for school, Tim was in his high chair finishing off his Cheerios. Jeanette had to run downstairs to put clothes in the dryer, so she said to him, "I'll be right back." A minute later she ran up the stairs and peeked around the corner at him. "Peekaboo," she said.

"Hi, Mama," he said with a big smile.

She walked toward him. "Tim, do you want a kiss?"

"Okay," he said.

Jeanette bent over and kissed his cheek, and as she did, he reached out his arms and hugged her.

As he finished his juice, he asked, "Where's 'Shell?"

"Michelle went to school."

Jeanette got him out of the high chair and took him into the family room. He sat on the floor at her feet, very quiet and looking tired. Dancing an Ernie doll toward him, she said, "Here comes Ernie to say hi to you."

He looked away. Then he sneezed and right away said, "Sorry."

Jeanette picked up a small, yellow school bus and offered it to him. "No," he said, hiding his eyes. "Please. Wanna see Daddy. Please! Need coat."

About ten days later Jeanette took Tim to the county building, where they connected with the caseworker. They were to meet with the parents, and Jeanette was apprehensive. The day before at the doctor's office, she had sat in the waiting room watching the door, knowing that the parents were aware of Tim's appointment and might walk in.

As soon as she noticed a young couple enter the lobby, she saw instant recognition on their faces. They came rushing over and the mother picked up Tim. "How are you, Tim? Are you okay?"

Tim quietly nodded.

Jeanette didn't want to act possessive so said nothing, quietly riding with them on the elevator to the cafeteria. Finding a table, they sat down with the caseworker.

Suddenly the father turned to Jeanette. Seething, he demanded, "I have just one question for you. What does Tim call you?"

In the training sessions we had been told that children naturally called foster parents Mommy and Daddy, and that it was good and helpful. Jeanette hesitated briefly, and the social worker said, "You won't like her answer."

Jeanette looked at his angry face. "Yes, he calls me Mommy," she said. "But Tim calls lots of people Mommy. When he sees pictures in magazines, he calls them Mommy."

The father was furious. "Don't you ever let him call you Mommy! When I was a boy, I didn't have a dad. He's got to know who his mommy and daddy are. Find something else for him to call you!"

Jeanette empathized with the young man, who obviously loved his son and struggled with old wounds. The meeting was soon over, and the young couple stood and watched as Jeanette and Tim got into the elevator and pushed the down button.

About a week later the social worker came to take Tim to live with an aunt and uncle. Jeanette sent with him some toys and a couple of new outfits. After they pulled out of the driveway, Jeanette cried.

In the days that followed, Jeanette very uncharacteristically woke up at night weeping. She felt so sorry for the boy. His mere two and a half weeks with our family had powerfully affected us.

chapter eight

*I*n contrast to Tim's sad departure, it was a celebration when our second foster child, a beautiful baby girl, left us to join her new family. Valerie had been with us four months and now was being adopted by a Christian couple with two young birth children. One Sunday we met them at St. John's Lutheran Church for Valerie's baptism. We were to be her godparents!

As we participated in the service, I remembered as a boy reciting the Apostle's Creed in St. Paul's Lutheran Church in Camden. Now Valerie would be raised with these same ringing affirmations. I looked at the stained-glass windows, the hundreds of worshipers, Valerie and her new family next to us, and my own three children beside me. How good to be part of all this.

Together we walked to the front. Before the pastor began, we were surprised that the parents handed Valerie to me to hold during the sacrament. There I stood, in my arms this little girl with fair cheeks and hair, so much like Michelle at that age. As we helped dedicate this precious child to God, I felt a sense of participating in something the Lord was doing marvelously well.

After the service, we all went to Valerie's new home to celebrate both her baptism and her adoption. We felt a unique bond with her and her family.

~

While Valerie was still living with us, the state agency had called with a special request. "Jeanette, we know you're a nurse, and we have a child with Down's syndrome. He needs a lot of work. This is probably longer-term foster care."

When they brought Billy to our home, we found out what she meant. He sagged forward on the family room floor and crawled across it like an inchworm. When we put him in the high chair, he couldn't sit up. Jeanette couldn't even steady him with one arm but had to use both arms to get him upright.

At fifteen months his development was greatly delayed. In fact, the medical people said it had been years since they'd last seen a Down's syndrome child that far behind. His mother, Laura, though she loved him, had been so timid and overwhelmed that she had been afraid to touch him.

Somehow from the beginning she had gotten wrong information. The doctor had used the word *mongoloid,* and Laura thought that was fatal. As she cared for her baby, she was always thinking he was about to die.

To feed Billy, Jeanette had to angle the spoon in his mouth a certain way, and every activity was a form of therapy. Several times a week she drove him to a medical center for evaluation and training. Therapy three times a day was a major challenge. Billy needed to get his belly off the floor and creep instead of crawl, to strengthen his abdominal muscles. But as Jeanette tried to get him up on his knees, he resisted. He hated the process, crying and getting hot and sweaty. Sometimes Greg would hold a colorful, noisy toy four feet in front of him, enticing him forward. Jeanette would hang on to keep him from sagging.

I would have been numb from all this, but Jeanette was excited about the challenge. She knew nothing about Down's syndrome, but she knew where to get help and she vigorously pursued the regimen. A month after Billy arrived, three medical workers told her, "We see such an improvement since a month ago. He's happier, brighter, stronger. He's holding himself up better and doesn't throw his head back when you pick him up."

This was gratifying, and when Laura started visits at our house, Jeanette showed her what she would eventually have to do when she got him back. On the floor behind Billy, Jeanette vigorously pulled back on his hips, urging him to move his knees forward without letting his belly sag. As usual Billy hated it, but despite his crying Jeanette kept at it until they finished.

Laura was upset, amazed at Billy's resistance and how much work therapy was. "I could never do that," she said. "I don't want to make him cry."

Jeanette looked at this pretty, dark-haired woman who worked at Taco Bell but often called in sick. She loved Billy, but that might not be enough. "Well, if we don't do this," Jeanette said, "he'll never learn to walk."

All through the spring, summer, and fall Jeanette kept at the therapy, and Billy became like a member of our family. He stayed in Greg's room and the two became buddies. Billy was difficult and stubborn but he was also responsive and fun. Jeanette developed a wonderful relationship with Billy's mother, trying to help her with her chaotic life.

At Christmas, because of activities and travel, Jeanette slacked off the therapy a bit, and after the holidays she saw a distinct difference. When Laura was there for a visit, Jeanette mentioned this to her. "Boy, did Billy ever regress. The past two weeks we didn't do as much therapy. Looks like we simply can't let up."

Laura was shocked. Not only did she fear she couldn't do the exercises, she realized they were absolutely necessary.

Soon after that, in a lengthy conversation with the caseworker, Jeanette said, "I think Laura would give him up for adoption. She's racked by guilt over the right thing to do as his mother, but she's overwhelmed."

The caseworker nodded and at their next meeting reported that she had asked Laura, "Have you ever thought about someone else raising Billy?"

"Yes, I have," Laura had responded. "I don't think I can take care of him."

A wonderful Christian family uniquely suited for a Down's syndrome child soon began the process of adopting Billy. But when it came time for Billy to leave, breaking the bond was difficult, especially for Greg, who had spent so much time with him the past year. The day he was to leave, none of our birth children wanted to go to school. They hated to say good-bye, and after that Greg never wanted to even talk about Billy.

At that point the emotional strains of foster care raised questions. Was all this worth it? Should we put our family through these wrenching farewells? The children stayed so long that they became part of our family, but then were torn away.

Yet now we had two friendships through Billy's time with us. We got to know the adoptive mother and were amazed at her pluck and resourcefulness. And we continued our friendship with Laura, who expressed great appreciation for all Jeanette had done. A few years later she invited us to her wedding. We met her Hispanic groom, witnessed the ceremony in his Catholic church, and mixed with a large crowd of relatives from both sides. We still receive Christmas cards from Laura with photos of her growing family, and we've stayed connected with Billy and his adoptive mother.

The day before Valerie was to leave—Billy was still with us— Jeanette said to our current caseworker, "I heard on the radio that you have a desperate need for homes for black boys."

"We certainly do."

Jeanette smiled. "So if you ever need a home for a black newborn, call me."

Actually, she was thinking of the distant future and was totally surprised when just two hours later the caseworker was on the phone. "Jeanette, we have a two-week-old black boy. He needs to be placed immediately."

"You're kidding!"

"Can you take him this afternoon? It will likely be short-term, since the grandmother plans to take him as soon as her home is approved."

That made it less jarring.

We were licensed for only two foster children, which meant we couldn't have more than two kids overnight. "But if you can get the adoptive mom to pick up Valerie tonight," the caseworker said, "I can bring him over this afternoon."

Jeanette grimaced at the rigid DCFS rules but said she'd call her back. The first thing she did was call me; then she went up to Todd's room. The rules said that a boy, even a newborn, had to room with another boy, so this baby couldn't be with Michelle. Greg already had Billy, so that left Todd.

She looked around at his small bedroom, jam-packed but neatly organized. "What would you think about having a little baby in your room? Could you make room for a portacrib?"

"No way!" Todd said immediately. He had his posters and gear just as he liked it. "There's no room! It wouldn't fit."

Jeanette shrugged her shoulders. "Well, the crib is upstairs. Look around. If you don't think it will work, we won't get him."

About fifteen minutes later Todd came downstairs and cheerfully said, "Okay, I've got the portacrib in there. I moved some stuff and made room."

His decision was to change our lives forever.

Next Jeanette called Valerie's adoptive mother and asked if she could take Valerie right away instead of the next day. "I guess I could," she said, both flustered and excited. Her husband was out of town and she was in the middle of preparations.

"How about seven o'clock?"

She agreed.

At four o'clock the caseworker arrived with the baby. Jeanette nearly cried when she saw him. "He's adorable," she said, touching his thick, soft curls and looking into his big eyes. Mellow and tiny, Ricky was in a yellow cotton sleeper and a thin blanket.

Jeanette enjoyed having such a young baby to care for, and she was amazed when in just a few days he looked her in the eyes and gave her an unmistakable smile.

Within a month, as the caseworker had said, his grandmother took him in. But she was already caring for his older brother, so after a few weeks she said it was too much for her. Ricky came back to the porta-crib in Todd's room.

Our street has at its cul-de-sac a big, grassy area large enough for all the neighbors to gather there with their picnic tables and lawn chairs. Every Fourth of July all twenty-two families participate in the annual Marion Court Pig Roast. Kids ride bikes, shoot baskets, and throw water balloons while adults watch and feast on pork and casseroles, salads and desserts.

We enjoyed our neighbors and found they were fully supportive of our having a black foster child. They welcomed Ricky without hesitation. That is, all except one.

Gladys was the neighbor from whom we'd borrowed the crib for Tim. She thought it was wonderful that we were taking care of foster kids. Jeanette enjoyed her animated, humorous personality and talked to her almost every day. More than once she had called Jeanette about a sick child, and Jeanette had rushed over. When Gladys called her to come see her new car, Jeanette crossed the street to share in the excitement.

So it was natural that the first day we had Ricky, Jeanette wrapped him in a blanket, carried him across the street, and rang her doorbell. "Look what I have, Gladys," she announced as she uncovered little Ricky for her to see.

"Oh, no!" she said, horrified. "Now you've really done it!"

From then on Gladys wouldn't let her children come on our property. If she saw Jeanette walking Ricky in a stroller, she would call her kids in. She wouldn't let them touch Ricky or get near him. Yet she continued to be very friendly with Jeanette.

Later Gladys got pregnant again, and Jeanette offered to return her crib and portacrib.

"No, I don't want them."

Because of her tone of voice, Jeanette asked, "Is it because a black baby slept in them?"

She hesitated, then finally admitted, "Yes."

Jeanette wasn't the only one who couldn't believe her attitude. Gladys's own mother was mortified, saying to her daughter, "What's got into you? I can't believe this. You were raised in Chicago in a mixed neighborhood. Gladys, where did you get this terrible attitude?"

Where indeed?

But then one day when Rick was about a year old, he was sitting on the sidewalk next to Jeanette when Gladys came by. "Rick was so irresistible," Jeanette told me later. "His whole face burst into a smile. And Gladys just couldn't resist. She finally picked him up and told me,

'You know, it's probably a good thing you got him. I can see he's just like every other kid.'"

When Rick was fifteen months old, it was time for him to leave. Our family once again had to deal with a loss. Now it was Todd's turn to lose a roommate to whom he had grown close. He found it very hard to say good-bye to Rick.

Jeanette and I also found things hard as we tried to stay afloat in foster care turmoil and a new reality: turbulent adolescence.

Todd had always struggled in school, and high school increased the pressures. For instance, his French teacher called and said only on one condition would she pass Todd with a D: he would have to promise not to take French II. We worried when he began wearing his hair long, reading Stephen King, and wearing black shirts. Todd would argue vehemently with Jeanette, and I would get caught between them.

Michelle was an honor student, gymnast, and school "Topperette." We believed that everything was going great for her, until she and Jeanette took a walk one spring night.

As they passed the nearby junior high, Michelle said, "Mom, I can't believe I did this."

"What?"

"At the party. I ate so many cookies and cake and felt so stuffed, I went and threw up."

Jeanette stopped in midtrack. She knew what that could mean. "Oh, honey! Don't do that."

"Oh, I know, Mom. That was awful. I'd never do that again."

But several months later we realized Michelle had begun some very unhealthy habits. We sought professional help and connected with an excellent young therapist. At the first meeting Jeanette and I were shown a film on eating disorders. It was chilling; we knew we were in for serious days ahead.

Although Michelle continued to excel through the rest of high school, she struggled with her eating problems and was so stressed out from studies and activities that she simply slept on the floor so she wouldn't have to make her bed. Tension at times was high. Michelle, like Todd, would argue with Jeanette—again with me in the middle. Jeanette felt that I didn't come down hard enough on the kids; I felt, with my different parenting style, that I shouldn't be just her enforcer. All this did nothing good for our marriage.

Fortunately, Greg was still happily playing with action figures and Legos.

The babies added to the stress, but they also gave Jeanette and Michelle a way to connect and have fun together. They needed that bridge.

Yet for me, foster care felt like chaos. This was heightened by our agreeing that the babies were Jeanette's project, not mine. I had been fully involved with our birth children, but with the foster kids I took a passive role. The strategy sounded good—I would do publishing and writing, she would do foster care. But the realities of home life pulled me in, and that put us both on edge. For me, babies in the house with adolescents was a volatile mix. More than once I told Jeanette, "These are the worst days of our marriage."

The question kept surfacing: Should we be doing foster care? Everyone had a breaking point. Were we stretching ourselves into much deeper chaos?

Yet if we couldn't care for these children, who could? It's never convenient to do something like foster care. Scores of babies were being warehoused in hospital cribs; children were moved from one emergency foster home to another. If anyone had the worst of chaos, it was these bereft children. And if Jeanette was called to this ministry, how could we ignore the agency's calls for help?

After Rick left, we were four months without foster children. Then DCFS placed a cocaine baby with us. Her name was Melody, and she had just spent three weeks in the hospital.

When she arrived, she still had cocaine effects. Her eyes appeared dazed; she had frequent tremors in her arms and legs. When Jeanette held her, she would stiffen her little black body and throw her head back. She also had eye and urinary tract infections.

Every six hours around the clock, Jeanette gave her an exact dose of medication. Melody also needed frequent blood tests. Jeanette loved having her nursing skills engaged, charting the medicines, monitoring the baby's progress, and conferring with doctors, including specialists in Chicago. Melody soon had less frequent tremors and a little better eye contact.

At this time our family had received a weeklong Caribbean cruise as a gift. Michelle, Todd, and Greg were ecstatic. Jeanette, who got seasick on boats, was not. So she packed the four of us off, saying Melody might be gone when we got back.

We had a wonderful time on the ship and the islands. In the Dominican Republic we visited a school with hundreds of lively children who eagerly gathered around us.

Somehow, exploring, I got separated from the others. I was gazing out at the ocean when a woman, perhaps a teacher, quietly called to me. She was saying something about a baby.

I was caught off guard and didn't understand. She kept talking until finally I realized she was offering me a child.

I shook my head no and she instantly disappeared.

Her disappearance made me feel the way I had years before when the woman in Chicago had locked her eyes on mine. What had just happened? Was she offering her own baby? Why me?

The schoolyard was full of smiling black children, all poor but relatively privileged. On this bleak island deeper poverty and desperation were common. Was this a mother's hope for her baby's survival? Something else? And I couldn't block the thought: *If these were white children, people would be flooding down here to adopt.*

When we arrived back at O'Hare Airport, Jeanette was waiting for us with a stroller. Inside, a plaid blanket covered a baby.

Michelle glanced at the stroller and said, "Oh, you still have Melody." But then Michelle did a double take. "Who's this?"

While we were gone, Melody had been returned to relatives. In the stroller was a seven-week-old black boy named Kwame, who was to have an enormous impact on our entire family.

chapter nine

While we were on the cruise, Jeanette had carefully packed for the departing Melody a basket full of clothes, supplies, diapers, and bottles, with meticulous instructions about her medications. But she had little hope that her efforts would make much difference as the baby reentered her birth world.

The next day Jeanette was to pick up Kwame. She drove to an emergency foster home in the suburbs and upon entering saw five or six young children wandering around the house. The foster mother led her to a sofa where a baby boy sat in an infant seat. *What a scrawny little kid,* Jeanette thought. *What straight hair.*

Right away she moved to lift him, but the foster mother said, "I don't pick these babies up much. It just spoils them."

What had the woman said? Jeanette was dumbfounded. Was this how the children were treated?

For the next couple of weeks, every time Jeanette would touch little Kwame, he would startle. But she kept holding him and soon he responded. In fact, she found him to be the most skin-hungry baby she had ever held. He couldn't get enough cuddling and hugging.

One day Jeanette and I drove into Chicago and parked our station wagon beside high mesh fences. Across the street was a massive gray building, the courthouse where for the first time we were to meet Kwame's mother.

We got Kwame out of his car seat, walked through the parking lot, and followed the flow of people into the building. A man seated by the metal detector started to wave me around, figuring I was a lawyer or social worker, but I shook my head no and followed the sets of bent shoulders ahead of me. Was I that obviously out of place here?

Maybe so. Instead of finding ourselves in a stately courtroom, we were walking into a huge warehouse with bay after bay holding about two hundred people each, all waiting for their turn with a judge. It reminded me of an old airport concourse in bad weather, thick with weary travelers waiting for late airplanes.

We located the proper bay; like the others, it was filled with people. Jeanette scanned the crowd, searching for the mother, who would be looking for us. Before long we saw a heavyset black woman walk in and look all around. Jeanette hurried over and brought her to our seats.

Anna was her name, and she was friendly, even thankful that Kwame was with us. We talked and sat and waited, like everyone else. The caseworker appeared, then scurried off to another case in another bay. We waited for the child advocate and the judge. Everything had to be ready for those very brief moments with his honor.

When we were finally called in, I was amazed at the brief, super-ficial procedure. The judge made a temporizing decision and set a new date. Then we were out of there.

Nothing had really happened. It was one more illustration of har-ried social workers and judges in a collapsing foster care system that jerked children back and forth, a system thrashing around in terminal agony.

An example of the results was baby Melody. After she left our home, I had asked Jeanette, "How do you think little Melody's doing?"

"Dead," she had answered, shaking her head. "I think she's dead. Or soon will be. That's what the social worker thinks. That's what I think. Everyone knows that the rehab programs don't work, but the mothers get the babies back anyway."

I knew that not far from this cavernous court building was a hos-pital with scores of unwanted black babies. Babies ready to bond and love, stuck in hospital cribs, destined for the system because they weren't the right color.

Kwame won the hearts of everyone in our family and church, bringing a great mixture of both joy and agony. He was supposed to spend a short time with us, then go back to Anna. But the months went by and before we knew it, he was celebrating his first birthday with us. Jeanette invited Anna to have a birthday dinner with us, and she joined us for an enjoyable evening.

Scrawny and very smart, Kwame would smile and probe with his knowing eyes and wheedle anything out of us. We all enjoyed the charisma of this child with the rich ebony skin. In our photo album are shots of Kwame at a neighbor's cookout, pictures of birthday celebrations, and photos of both his parents sitting at our kitchen table.

Jeanette kept reaching out to Anna, talking to her on the phone and trying to help her get stable enough to have Kwame back. Anna needed furniture for her apartment, so Jeanette volunteered to buy some for her at a garage sale. Anna was enthusiastic, and Jeanette found a dresser, desk, chair, bookcase, and table.

I helped her load all this stuff into our station wagon, which was really not adequate to carry it all. "This is dangerous," I said, "to drive on the tollway with this stuff blocking the mirrors." But Jeanette—farmer's daughter and driver of tractors—said, "I'll drive carefully." And off she went. She and Anna's teenage son lugged the furniture up to the second floor.

Yet even though Kwame's parents had visited our home twice, the relationship with them was deteriorating as the system ground on. Kwame knew all about his birth parents, but to a little boy who has known and bonded with only one family, they must have seemed irrelevant. It was into my arms that he ran and leaped when I'd come home. It was Jeanette who would feed him and rock him and laugh at his antics. It was Michelle and Todd and Greg who played with him, took him to the park, read him stories. How could he think of himself as any different from our birth children, who also had started out their lives in a Myra crib?

It was when Jeanette and I were on a trip in Wisconsin that we got terrible news about Kwame. At home Michelle was baby-sitting him, and he seemed sick, had a fever, and was becoming lethargic. Jeanette called home to check on him twice a day, and Sunday evening when

Kwame seemed no better, she told Michelle, "Call the doctor's office as soon as it opens on Monday."

Early Monday morning there was no answer at home, so Jeanette called the doctor. He said Kwame had been brought in and was very sick. They had rushed him to a specialist. Jeanette then dialed the specialist, who said, "It's good you called. We've done a spinal tap. He probably has spinal meningitis. Your daughter is crying and very upset. We've sent him by ambulance to the hospital."

Jeanette looked grim as she put down the phone and said in a tight voice, "It's serious. Extremely serious."

We threw our things into suitcases and bolted to the car. In a few hours we were walking into a room in the children's ward. Kwame lay in a coma amid tubes and monitors.

"He may not live through the night," the doctor told us. "He's a very sick little boy."

Jeanette stayed with him while I went home to be with the kids. Kwame lived through the night, but the next morning he was still deep in a coma. The specialist gave us a litany of sobering news: "He may very well die. If he survives, he will probably lose his sight and hearing."

A cot was moved into his room so Jeanette could stay with him round the clock. Kwame's parents came by train from the city for a brief visit.

Five different doctors were working on the case, and most of them saw Kwame each day. Standing by Kwame's crib, the main specialist told Jeanette, "He won't come out of this with everything intact. He's had a stroke. He is paralyzed on one side, is blind and deaf, and has a bleeding stress ulcer. He may not survive."

Jeanette felt tears as she stared at Kwame's little face. A mother sometimes feels the strongest bonds with the child most deeply hurt. As Jeanette slept on the cot beside him day and night, checking his IV and vital signs and repositioning him in the bed, she felt an ever-deepening love for this helpless little boy.

However, Kwame's father, Walter, saw Jeanette as an intruder. Greatly upset after the doctor described his son's extreme condition, he telephoned Jeanette in a rage, insisting he be moved to Children's

Memorial Hospital in Chicago. "How did you let him get this, anyway?" he demanded. "He was at your house!" He accused her of not
taking proper care of him. The ironic thing was that Jeanette, as an RN,
scheduled health care fanatically. The schedule for the meningitis
immunization was then at eighteen months of age; Kwame was hos-
pitalized when he was seventeen months old.

The angry father was not about to listen. "We're going to have him
transferred," he said. "We're coming to get him!"

The social workers said he would do no such thing. The doctors
said that moving him would be foolish. The hospital put security
guards on alert. Jeanette was very nervous, but that night Walter didn't
show up.

Nor did he the next night. Kwame meanwhile was slowly coming out of his coma. Jeanette would sit hour after hour rocking him,
the IV tube attached to his arm. She would carefully put him in a little red wagon and pull him with his IV down the hospital corridor.

Gradually he started to see a bit. Little by little he started hearing
things. Jeanette coaxed the skinny little boy to eat some baby food. Each
day Kwame made a tiny bit of progress. People in our church, and con-
tacts all over the world, were praying for him. Even Billy Graham sent
me a telegram assuring me he was praying for our foster son.

Jeanette was staying at the hospital, so I sent her a fun card showing a nurse sewing up an injured teddy bear. I wrote, "You really are
amazing, the way you cope so positively and know just how to handle
everyone from Kwame's parents to the doctors. May your energy and
good spirits continue. Hang in there!"

She needed our encouragement. She stayed fifteen days and nights
in the hospital, loving and praying and nursing him toward recovery.
At the end of that time the doctors were amazed at how steadily he
was getting better. He could see, he could hear, he could even smile.
Though he still needed lots of therapy, a pediatric neurologist said,
"This kid is a miracle. I'm *so* surprised he came out of this so well."

The day before his release, relatives from Norway arrived. It was a
festive time the next day when Jeanette brought home the boy we had
feared would die. My cousin Hjordis and her husband, Johan, plus

neighbors, family, and friends celebrated with balloons and streamers and cake and Norwegian goodies.

Jeanette had fed, bathed, and exercised Kwame in the hospital and had kept track of his medications. Now she had a full summer ahead of physical therapy. The illness became a powerful bonding experience for Jeanette—and for all of us. By the end of summer Kwame had made a complete, miraculous recovery.

But it was a sad turning point with his birth parents. Walter grew hostile. He hated losing control over his son. He hated the DCFS system, and he hated his son's being raised by a white woman. He told her he had thrown out the window all the furniture Jeanette had brought to Anna. And Anna had always been unstable, suffering from asthma, high blood pressure, and a psychiatric disorder. We began to fear that maybe it hadn't been such a good idea to have them visit Kwame at our house.

And Rick? After sixteen months with us he was gone but not forgotten. We cherished a little card that Ann, our caseworker, had sent us when Rick went back to Jean, his birth mother. It read:

> Dear Myra Family,
>
> Words cannot express our gratitude for everything you have done for Ricky. You have given him a fresh, loving, nurturing start. He will be the best he can be because of what you have done for him. God will watch over him and protect him. I hope you will call and see him.
>
> Love,
> Ann and Ricky (Future President
> of the United States)

That little note expressed our hopes: that God would watch over and protect him. And Jeanette took seriously the encouragement to be a "significant other" in Rick's life. She continued her good relationship with Jean and with others in the family. They all wanted her to maintain contact with Rick.

One Friday she drove to Jean's apartment and picked him up for the weekend. Ours was his original home but now he came only occasionally. He eagerly entered our house and began exploring. I watched as he went downstairs, investigating everything in the kids' playroom.

"What's in there?" he asked, pointing to the closed doors to my den.

"Books and a desk. That's where I work. Want to see?"

I opened the door for him and let him go in. He looked at the chairs, a painting of prehistoric animals, and some photos. But what really caught his eye were brightly colored children's books on a shelf.

"What are they?" he asked.

"Books." I pulled several off the shelf, and his hand shot out to grab *Serendipity,* which had a bright-pink sea dragon on the cover. He fingered the book as if he'd never seen one before.

"Want me to read it to you?"

He climbed into my lap and surrendered the book to me, but his eyes were glued on the bright, lovable dragon on the cover. Serendipity had been born in the Arctic all alone, an innocent soul in search of identity. She asked a walrus and a dolphin who she was, but they couldn't tell her. No one could explain, and not until the end of the book did she learn her true purpose and identity.

Rick barely moved as I read and turned the pages. When I finished, he reached out and reopened it.

"Want me to read it again?"

He nodded yes, and I think he would have had me read it ten more times if I had offered. He wanted to know if he could carry it, so then he wandered the house, pink dragon book in hand. Here he was "back home," yet now he came from a totally different world. Perhaps he was as perplexed as Serendipity was.

Later as I was helping Rick get on his pj's, he asked me a question that caught me off guard. In fact, I felt as if I were hearing a line from a TV show when this little boy asked, "Can I call you Dad?"

I felt torn. For sixteen months he'd been our foster baby, but now for a long time he had lived with his birth family. What good would it do him to call me Dad? Would it raise false expectations? Sure, I could be Dad to him several weekends a year and maybe at Christmas. But would that really help him? He needed a real dad if he was to find himself, as Serendipity had at the end of the book.

Rick was looking into my face—he'd always had good eye contact. "Sure, Rick, you can call me Dad. That's fine." But I had no idea what that might mean as I lifted him into my arms, gave him a hug, and said, "Good night, little guy."

chapter ten

*O*ne Sunday morning Rick was again with us for the weekend, and we set off for church. I parked the car in the lot, then unbuckled his car seat. He jumped out and when I reached for his hand, he took it with a smile.

As we walked toward the entrance, he held my fingers tight. "You gonna leave me alone?" he asked.

I knew that he'd been left alone lots of times and that it had become his greatest fear. Many times when he'd see Jeanette or me putting on a coat, he'd ask that same question.

"No, Rick, I won't leave you alone." I lifted him into my arms and carried him. As we got closer to the church, he asked me again. "You gonna leave me alone?"

"Never. I will never leave you alone, Rick." But I knew that most of the time he wasn't with our family and that others would leave him alone.

Inside the church Rick sat quietly during the service until he saw a boy being baptized. He asked, "Could I go up there and do that, too?"

He simply wanted to go where the action was and to be special, having no idea what baptism was all about. But his question made me realize that somehow it might be in my hands as to whether this child would ever be baptized or find a life of faith.

In providing foster care, we had not been remotely thinking of adoption. But short of that, this little boy who was now bonded to our family had little hope. Magazines kept putting in my face devastating statistics about what was happening to black males in America. Drugs. Jail. Death.

As the choir sang, I put my arm around Rick. The odds were hugely stacked against him: a violent welfare neighborhood, no father at home, two uncles murdered.

And it was counterproductive to keep shifting Rick back and forth between two contrasting worlds. It was getting harder and harder to take him back to his apartment. As Jeanette would drive to within a few blocks so that Rick recognized the neighborhood, he would start puckering up and tears would flow. By the time they reached the parking lot, Rick would be hysterical. Once Jeanette had to call on adults to help her pry Rick's protesting little body from the car.

One day when Jeanette visited Jean's apartment, Jean asked to be taken across town. As they rode, Jean came up with a suggestion: "Ricky keeps saying, 'Call Jeanette.' He loves coming to your house. Could you take him for a couple years, while I get back to school and get a job?"

Jeanette knew that in their community people would live with relatives for extended periods. Yet she also knew that it would be traumatic for Rick to be rooted in our community, then go back. "Jean, I couldn't do that," Jeanette told her. "No way. We couldn't give him back after having him for two years."

Jean didn't say anything. Jeanette kept driving, thinking about Rick and his tears. Finally she said, "Want me to keep him forever?"

Without hesitating Jean said, "Yeah, you can do that. You had him when he was a baby."

Jeanette nodded. "Our family loves him," she said. Then she asked, "You want us to adopt him?"

Jean had apparently been thinking about this and quickly said that our adopting Rick was a good idea. But Jeanette said just as quickly, "Oh, I've got to talk to Harold about this."

Later when we did talk, Jeanette largely dismissed the conversation. "She'll never do it," she said. "She'll never actually sign the papers."

I didn't know whether to be relieved at that or saddened. I wanted the best for Rick, but I was far from pressing that we adopt him.

One day on Christmas week I was home caring for both Kwame and Rick, who loved playing together. I decided to drive them to the nearby Indian Lakes Resort, which had a special Christmas display. We were bundled tightly against the snow, and I led them through the parking lot and the big glass doors of the entrance.

Inside the high atrium was a magical world of decorated bridges, sparkling trees, a sleigh full of presents. We walked over each bridge, inspected the gala sleigh, arced our necks to look up at the Santa far above our heads.

The children's book about Santa that I'd started in that donut shop emphasized that the original Saint Nicholas had "loved Jesus very much." Now we talked about Christmas and Saint Nick. But as I walked with these boys, I wondered. Rick would go back to Jean in a few days with his Christmas toys and a couple of new outfits. And Kwame's future was a great confusion.

Jeanette and I knew that transracial adoption was highly controversial. I had been amazed to learn how viscerally the National Association of Black Social Workers condemned it. They and the NAACP accused whites like us who adopted black children of being guilty of "blatant cultural genocide." The organizations were reacting to instances of black mothers unfairly losing their children to whites and of kids raised with little preparation for life in a black skin.

On the other hand, significant studies showed that black children raised by whites generally grew up to be healthy, well-adjusted adults. And for thousands of children it was a choice of white parents or the devastating foster care system.

We were whipsawed by this. In our concern to share our love and God's love, might we only make things worse? Would children we adopted be denied an ethnic heritage vital to their well-being? Would our divided, embittered society create ever larger chasms of enmity we could never bridge?

One evening Jeanette and I sat in a small semicircle of white suburban adults. All were considering transracial adoption. Across from us sat a tall, fiftyish black man with an intent gaze and a professional demeanor. Mel Copeland, a school counselor, was supportive of such adoptions when other alternatives were unavailable. He told us of the racism we would encounter and of recent incidents in our local schools, in stores, and even in the courts. No, racism was not dead in the suburbs.

Then he asked us a sobering question. His eyes swept across each face in the room as he asked in sharp tones, "Who are you, that you think *you* can raise a black child?"

Like confrontational song lyrics, the question hung in my mind. Who indeed was I? Nordic white, for one thing! How could I be Dad to a descendant of black slaves? Were we being presumptuous?

Yet Rick, a boy we loved, was at a crossroads. Everyone involved, including his relatives, was urging us to bring him into our family. We had to decide, one way or the other.

With all the challenges in my life, was I foolish to consider stretching myself this far? At work, every time I thought the demands would ease off, some new crisis would arise.

For instance, one morning Duncan Brown called. Billy Graham was concerned about withering critiques he had heard about *Christianity Today*. As founder of the magazine and as CTI's chairman, Billy was rightly interested in ensuring the magazine's vitality and integrity. Strong academic voices were saying that it had lost its original, prophetic voice—that the glory had departed. Just when the church was being swamped by culture, critics said, CT was capitulating, CT was embracing shallow populism.

Christianity Today had always evoked passionate, contrasting opinions. One option on the table during the 1975 crisis had been to allow its circulation to drift down to thirty thousand and let it be a smaller, subsidized journal. That plan was rejected in favor of a publication paying its own way and seeking maximum readership. But that meant attracting readers—publishing a magazine that a hundred and fifty thousand people would pay for.

Over the years we believed we had struck a balance, not sacrificing integrity but communicating to a broad audience. C. S. Lewis was a model. From the simplicity of his Narnia series to his classics such as *Mere Christianity*, Lewis combined depth with accessibility.

The critics, of course, would say we were a far, far cry from Lewis. To deal with the strategic questions, we brought a blue-ribbon group of theologians and evangelical leaders together, and we discussed the issues in our board. One conclusion reached was that I needed to give daily, hands-on leadership to the editors.

But how would I find time for that? We were now publishing lots of magazines and copublishing books, growing in many directions. The demands for high-quality inquiry and precisely nuanced editing in *Christianity Today* magazine were steep.

Soon I was working out of two offices in our building, one editorial and one administrative. Although the process ultimately worked out well and the staff grew into mature and effective responsibility, I felt thoroughly strung out.

Yet I couldn't ignore Rick's needs. I asked myself, *How did Jesus set his priorities?* With just three years in earthly ministry, he had little time to fulfill his Father's plans. How did children fit in? Despite all the pressures, when his disciples tried to shoo away children so he could do what they considered the real work, Jesus rebuked them.

What was my real work? What were the great and mighty things I was supposed to be doing?

Jesus said, "Suffer the little children to come unto me, and forbid them not: for of such is the kingdom of God" (Mark 10:14 KJV). If he was so vehement about children, how should I view them?

How valuable was Rick?

The song I'd sung often to my children at bedtime answered it:

Jesus loves the little children,
    All the children of the world.
Red and yellow, black and white,
    They are precious in his sight.

Even so, no one can plunge in and do everything. At my stage in life, adopting an African-American child was a magnificent opportunity, but one wrapped up in absurdly weighty commitments.

Was I, in my fifties, too old? Was it fair to the child? To me? And what stresses would this put on our marriage? Foster care had certainly brought plenty of them. My intense need for solitude was constantly being shoved aside, and the chaos of children's coming and going had roiled up stress that was punishing on my body.

About this time Jeanette and I saw the movie *Parenthood,* which in some ways mirrored the constant chaos in our house. The beleaguered Steve Martin, after a lot of crazy episodes and more pressure than any father should have to endure, was arguing with his wife, who had just told him something very disconcerting: she was pregnant again. Martin was thoroughly upset. How could he handle yet more parenthood stress?

The wife said, "What do you want me to give you? Guarantees? These are *kids,* not appliances."

Then Grandma entered the room. Obviously, she had heard their conversation, and she said with a twinkle in her eye, "You know, when I was nineteen, Grandpa took me on a roller-coaster ride. Up. Down. Up. Down. Oh, what a ride!"

Steve Martin gives her his disgusted look, but she keeps talking: "I always wanted to go again. You know, it was just interesting to me that a ride could make me so frightened, so scared, so excited, so thrilled— all together!"

As I listened in the theater to the old woman with the smile on her face, it struck me that this was just the right analogy. Like the movie's roller-coaster ride of parenthood, life was full of challenge and stress and outrageous situations, and maybe my only real choice was to enjoy the ride.

Steve Martin's mother-in-law then said about the roller coaster, "Some didn't like it. They went on a merry-go-round. That just goes around. Nothing. I like the roller coaster. You get more out of it."

Well, I wasn't sure I preferred the roller coaster at all—as it was obvious that Steve Martin did not. But I walked out of that theater challenged by the film's emphasis that someone had to take care of these children and that it was a messy, demanding, difficult thing—but also enormously, powerfully rewarding. In fact, strapping oneself in for the ride can result in the kind of joy that only love for children can create.

Not long after that Jeanette and I drove to a hotel in Wisconsin for a weekend to make the decision that would change our lives. We faced two questions.

First, how could we humbly, wisely discern what God was leading us to do?

This was far from simple. We kept being whipsawed by circumstances, one moment seeing positive signals and "coincidences" favoring adoption, then witnessing reversals that created doubt.

Second, Rick was now three and a half. What was truly best for him?

We planned to go over all the pros and cons, but somehow even before checking in I sensed it was inevitable. We were going to adopt Rick.

So after that weekend Jeanette called Jean's house. She wasn't there, nor was Rick. She'd gone to Mississippi, and her family didn't know if she'd be back. Talk about being whipsawed!

About three weeks later Jean called. Jeanette asked, "When did you get back from Mississippi?"

Jean said, "This morning. Come get your baby."

We'd had Rick for about a month when Jeanette said to Jean, "I should bring him back to you. Keep him for a week and think it over." Jean did so, and when the week was over and Jeanette came to pick him up, Jean still thought we should adopt him.

But Richard, the father, was at the house and he wasn't so sure. "He's my namesake," he told Jeanette. "I don't know if I should do this."

But Richard had been uninvolved and had shown no interest in his boy. Jeanette felt awkward, but she looked him in the eyes and said, "Somebody needs to give this kid love and food and clothes. Richard, are you going to feed him and provide for him and give him what he needs?"

He hesitated. "Well, I know you can do that." He paused and grinned. "Can I come, too?"

Jeanette grinned back, and Richard said, "I want to know what your husband says about all this. I want to meet this guy."

So some weeks later I took a lunch break and nailed down a table at Baker's Square, then waited for Jeanette to arrive with Jean and Richard. When they came in, I was impressed with how they made such a neat and good-looking couple. As we sat down and ate, we had a pleasant time and talked about what would be best for Rick.

"Our community is very white," Jeanette said. "Rick wouldn't have black playmates. Does that bother you, Richard?" He said that it didn't, and he had no questions to ask me.

Now all of Rick's relatives wanted us to adopt him.

After that it was a lengthy process with plenty of red tape and paperwork. Richard and Jean came three separate times to Wheaton to meet with a social worker to make sure they were well informed and comfortable with their decision. They seemed very happy about their little boy coming to live with us, and they readily signed the papers.

Finally Jeanette, Rick, and I were sitting before a Dupage County judge. During the proceedings he turned to me and asked, "Do you realize that if something happens to her"—he nodded toward Jeanette—"you would be responsible to raise this child?"

I said that yes, I was very much aware of that.

chapter eleven

*W*e were adopting Rick. But what about Kwame? Both boys were in our home, but as Rick's adoption progressed, Kwame's future became more confusing, both to him and to us. He feared the visits to his birth parents. Why was this happening to him? Why couldn't he just stay with us, the way Rick was?

The situation had been going back and forth for three years. One month Kwame was going home; the next he was staying awhile longer. When it was time for home visits, Kwame would scream and hang desperately onto Jeanette, then sob as the social worker drove him away.

We felt trapped and helpless against the system. Jeanette felt deep anger as Kwame became victimized by it. She had to be his advocate, working with a series of four different caseworkers.

One was particularly difficult. Although we'd had very good experiences with African-American social workers, this one obviously resented our having a black child in our home. As he brought Kwame back from a home visit one day, Jeanette asked him how court had gone.

"What do you mean, how did court go?" he demanded.

"Who was there? Did both birth parents come?"

"What is that to you?" he asked sarcastically. "I don't need to tell you that."

Jeanette was taken aback. "Look," she said steadily, "I'm just interested in whether he'll be returned next week or if we'll have him for two more years."

This was the only social worker who was gruff with Kwame and made no attempts to calm his fears. "It's none of your business," he said condescendingly. "I don't need to be cross-examined by you. You're just doing foster care."

Jeanette locked onto his eyes and said, "You and I are going to have a hard time working together."

"Why is that?"

"Because I'm not used to being talked to this way. You just don't understand. When these kids come into my house, I treat them as if they're one of my own kids. That's what a foster mom is supposed to do!"

Because of the worker's attitude we faced a maddening dilemma. For months our family had been planning to spend a full week in Wisconsin for Christmas. All our children were excited about it. But when Jeanette asked the social worker for the standard permission to take Kwame out of state, his immediate response was, "Oh, no. Kwame can't miss his visit with the family."

"The family won't mind," Jeanette said. "They've canceled visits lots of times. They'll want Kwame to have a good Christmas."

"No. It just can't be done. He's scheduled for a visit."

Jeanette couldn't believe it. "Just one two-hour visit?" she said. "For that you'd make him miss his Christmas trip? Kwame has been part of this family all his three years. How do you think he'll feel, not spending Christmas with the other kids? You'd rob him of that just for a visit that might get canceled anyway?"

But he wouldn't budge and wouldn't even ask the parents about it. We went to Wisconsin for the week without Kwame, who had to stay behind with a baby-sitter—at our expense, of course.

When we heard later that this social worker had been fired, we were not surprised. And not only did we keep getting new social workers, but the same was true of therapists. One who had worked with the mother for a year called Jeanette and said she was going to court to recommend that Kwame not be returned. She wanted to make sure we would be willing to keep him. But she left her job, and the next therapist said, "We have to give this family a chance." Anna during this time had had two more babies. When she didn't take her medicine, she would end up in a psychiatric hospital. Back and forth the signals went, one month the parents getting Kwame back, the next a new delay. And no matter how many lawyers and social workers we talked to, we were "only" the foster parents, with no say.

Yet we were the ones who lived with Kwame's fears of the home visits. When a social worker would arrive, Kwame would run and hide. He'd scream, "No! I not go there!"

Jeanette began feeling like a mother with a critically ill child on a respirator—knowing he was dying, but wondering when the plug would be pulled. Dragging out the process simply increased the trauma. She would say to the caseworker, "If you're returning him home, do it!"

At this time Fox TV had started a series called *Yearbook*. It followed about a dozen high schoolers with a video camera through their senior year. They chose our local high school, Glenbard West. Since the Desert Storm war was approaching, one of the seniors they chose was Todd, who had joined the marines and was attending reserve weekends.

As it looked more and more as if Kwame would go back to his birth parents, the camera crews would be in and out of our kitchen and up in Todd's bedroom interviewing him. It was also the time when on TV news shows and *Oprah* they were showing the clips of a little black girl being taken, screaming, from her white foster mother's arms. In our foyer the situation was similar. Kwame would dread the appearance of the caseworker. When he appeared at the front door, we knew we would have to physically force him to go. Todd, Greg, Rick, the TV cameras, all were in the foyer, all of us trying to reassure Kwame that it was okay, even when we felt at that moment that nothing was okay.

The segment of *Yearbook* was televised nationally on the Fox network, and for years none of us could stand to watch the part about Kwame being taken from us for a home visit. Here he was three years old—all he'd ever known was our family. This boy who would run into my arms at the slightest nod was told, "You won't live here anymore." Rick was staying, but Kwame was traumatized by having to go to people who to him were strangers.

His parents were rough on him, showing their anger that he lived with whites. Walter wrote us a note in Kwame's name, saying, "I have a proud *black* history. Please don't rob me of it. Don't take what was born in me away." Then he added, "It's not all your fault. I'm black and you just don't understand."

Of course we didn't understand—not in the depth in which only an African-American could. But neither did Kwame, who was only confused by their ramming his black heritage at him, as if everything were his fault.

What grieved us most was the dad's hostility. We learned that on visits he yelled at his son for mentioning our names. We wondered what else was happening when Kwame was there for forty-eight hours.

One afternoon after the caseworker brought Kwame back from a visit, Jeanette saw what looked like a slap mark on the two-year-old's cheek. As required, she took him to the pediatrician to document it. Six weeks later when bathing him after another visit, Jeanette noticed marks on his buttocks and the backs of his thighs. This time when she took him to the doctor, he said, "I have to call this in."

The next day an investigator came to our house, and when Jeanette opened the door, she thought, *Thank goodness she's black. At least Walter can't say this was white people making this up.*

The investigator checked the little guy over and said emphatically, "Those are belt marks. I am telling you he will not go for a visit until we get this straightened out."

When Walter was questioned, he was furious. He called Jeanette and said, "You've got Anna all upset. I don't know what happened; I've been at work all day." He interrogated Jeanette about who had sent in the report. She told him it was confidential. He bore in on her, insisting she tell him and saying she must have done it.

Finally, his voice bitter, Walter said, "All right, the gloves are coming off. I'm coming to get my son!" Click.

Jeanette stood with the phone in her hand, shaken. The call had come just as she was getting ready to go with me to an important CTI board dinner. She would be a hostess and had arranged for a baby-sitter, but now she wondered if she should go. It sounded as if Walter would be barging into our house before the hour was up.

She alerted me, and then she talked to our next-door neighbor, a fire chief. He said that if there was a problem, he'd rush right over. Jeanette gave detailed instructions for the sitter, including the emergency number 911 and the numbers of the neighbors we had alerted.

It turned out that Walter's threat had been empty, like the previous ones.

One day Jeanette was driving home from DCFS when Kwame asked, "Mommy, are you white?"

"Yes, I'm white."

"Mommy, Anna said you're white, Todd white, I black."

"Yes, and Ricky's skin is black. God made us all, and we have different skin colors."

"No!" Kwame yelled. "I not black! I white! I white like Todd! I white like you!" He sobbed hard and insisted, "No! I don't want to be black! I white like you! *I not black!*"

We had always been open about skin color and how God made all people beautiful. We knew that Kwame and Ricky would have plenty of identity issues to work through, and we agonized for Kwame that he was confronted by them so negatively.

Walter kept working to turn Kwame against us. He ridiculed the boy's prayers and the Sunday school songs he loved to sing. So Kwame was hearing that everything and everyone he had always loved was shameful.

Knowing that Kwame had to bond with his parents, we were always positive in what we said to him about them. "They are your mommy and daddy. They love you very much."

"No!" he would explode. "They not love me! Anna *not* my mommy!"

But Walter's messages were getting through. One night, after Kwame had a long visit with his parents, Jeanette was rocking him and singing to him at bedtime, as she always did. In the past Kwame had sung along and snuggled happily. But this time as she was rocking him and softly singing "Jesus Loves Me," Kwame pulled his head off Jeanette's shoulder, leaned back—and then he spit right in her face!

Jeanette reached for a tissue, stunned. As she wiped the spit off her face, she realized that the father must have told him to do that. She took comfort in a verse of Scripture: "My grace is sufficient for you, for my power is made perfect in weakness" (2 Cor. 12:9).

Yet she was being worn down. She said to me, "This is the worst agony! All the canceled visits, Walter's threats, Kwame upset and wanting hugs but the next minute throwing food, one professional saying he'll never return and another saying it's just a matter of time. Three years of this! It's ripping us apart."

Then came the final good-bye. We could barely stand it, knowing it would be the last time we would ever see him. We couldn't even send his favorite blanket or his small photo album—the father had previously sent back Christmas gifts we'd sent.

When the social worker pulled up in his station wagon, Kwame had run off to hide. Jeanette brought him to the foyer crying sadly, a clingy, hug-me-Mommy kind of crying.

I stood there helpless. Jeanette was holding Kwame, and the kids were all standing around not knowing what to do or say. Here I'd been Father to him all the three years he'd been alive, but I could do nothing. Wasn't a father supposed to protect his son?

I took aside the caseworker—a compassionate one we really liked—and asked, "What if their home situation falls apart again? What happens to Kwame then?"

He shrugged and lifted his eyes heavenward.

"Obviously," I said, "if Kwame goes back into foster care, we'd be called, wouldn't we? They'd check with us first, right?"

He sighed and shook his head. "Probably not."

"Probably not!" I'd been shocked before at the system, but this blew me away. "What do you mean, probably not? That's insane! The boy is bonded to us. We're emotionally and in every way his parents and family. From birth to three years old! We all know the research on bonding; for a child to heal, he would need to reconnect with the family he lived with his first three years!"

"You're absolutely right." His voice and body language were thoroughly sympathetic, but his words were unreal. "But bringing him back is very unlikely."

"Why not? What possible reason could there be?"

"They probably don't even have your name linked," he said. "They wouldn't even know how to find you."

Whaaat? Wouldn't know how to find us? How could that possibly be? The foster care system as a blunt instrument of unintended carnage loomed before me with Kafkaesque menace. Kwame's being shuttled off to another house full of strangers while the people bonded to him didn't even know—how absurdly tragic.

Yet I believed the caseworker.

We all hugged Kwame good-bye and told him we loved him very, very much. We could barely watch as the station wagon pulled out of the drive for the last time. It was a painful sundering.

In fact, it felt like a funeral. Our good friends Ray and Lois Badgero, who were also adopting black children, sent a dozen roses and a card on which Lois wrote, "We love you and *hurt* also when you are in pain. Know that we are here anytime for you." Prentiss, the wonderfully wise black caseworker who had helped us with Billy, sent a card that said, "I know that looks like a mountain up ahead of you. But if you just take it one step at a time, I know you'll make it. My thoughts and prayers are with you."

Over the following days we all kept wondering how Kwame was doing with his birth family. My subconscious must have been dealing with the loss, for a few weeks later I had a dream that summed up all my longings and sadness for him:

I am in my parents' home and see that Rick and other small children are playing by the upstairs windows. Michelle, beautiful, bright, and lively, is putting paint on their faces. She dabs on circles and streaks of bright colors. All the little kids are laughing with her and playing joyfully.

Suddenly I am downstairs and Kwame appears. He is walking up to me. Gone for several weeks, he seems totally changed. He has a blank expression and looks older. On his right cheek and jaw are three long white scars, as if a three-pronged rake has unevenly cut across his face.

I reach out and hug him but he does not respond. His not hugging back feels strange and unnatural.

Somehow he says—it's a voice that is hardly his—"They want to know if I can stay with you."

My heart rises. Have things changed? Could he be coming back?

I don't know how to respond. I feel so helpless. I gently hold his shoulders and say, "We'll have to see, Kwame. We'll have to see what can be done."

But before I can hug him again, the other children are all around us with their gaily painted faces.

Rick is standing in front of us, looking at Kwame, awkward, not knowing what to do.

I motion him closer. Rick starts forward, his rich brown skin contrasting with Kwame's pale face.

Then, like watching a wide-screen movie close-up, I see Rick putting his wonderfully painted face next to Kwame's wounded one. Rick is pressing his cheek to Kwame's, and my dream creates an extreme close-up on their faces tight together.

It's as if I'm in a theater, both young faces much larger than life, both looking right at me and filling my vision. As I watch, the bright colors from Rick's face—the reds and greens and yellows and blues edged with white—slowly begin to widen onto Kwame's cheek. But as the celebratory colors start spreading from one boy to the other, I awaken.

chapter twelve

Rick's adoption was a gala event. During a morning worship service, Jeanette, Rick, and I were invited up front. Pastor Bob Harvey, with his red hair, warm humor, and broad smile, prayed for us. As he did, I thought, *Contrasted with the heavenly Father, I'm inadequate. I'm white, not black. But the most powerful thing a father can do for any son is to point him to the heavenly Father.*

Afterward the congregation celebrated with punch and cupcakes topped with multicolored sprinkles and lots of helium balloons—several of which ended up tied to Rick's hand. Everyone gave the five-year-old lots of high fives.

We also designed and mailed a celebratory announcement to friends and relatives. In Florida Jeanette's dad was in the hospital and was proud to show the nurses a photo of his new grandchild. Michelle was in Kenya on a trip with fellow Gordon College students. Her professor, knowing about Rick, said repeatedly to the students, "This opens your eyes to a new world." When Michelle arrived back from Africa, she found her dorm room door covered with congratulations for having a new brother.

Friend Joe Palma, a calligrapher, painted on Rick's bedroom wall, "Jesus Loves Ricky."

We remained acutely aware of all the controversy about whites raising blacks. Yet we were equally aware of the many other boys who needed homes. I thought of all those babies in the Chicago hospital. I thought of the way newborns come into the world ready to give and receive love, but that these babies would lie there having no one with whom to bond. Children were jerked from foster home to foster home, with devastating results.

In an adoption support group for whites adopting blacks, we heard a common opinion that it was best to have more than one black child. Jeanette asked me, "Do you think we should raise just one black boy? Shouldn't he have a companion?"

"Maybe so," I said. "If we adopt a newborn out of the system, we might break the cycle for one child."

We felt that God was leading us to at least take initial steps and that our calling was to a healthy infant boy.

We had some wonderful caseworkers at DCFS, some black and some white. They all strongly encouraged us to get a black sibling for Rick. "Do it!" they said. "These babies need a home."

However, a call to a caseworker in Chicago revealed decidedly different viewpoints within the state agency. Jeanette was following up on a lead about a newborn, and the man who answered the phone was very short with her.

"Are you white?" he demanded.

"Yes."

"Oh, we would never place a healthy black infant with a white family. We'd have to look for a black family."

"How long would you have to look?"

"At least a year."

What a travesty! The idea of a baby in its first year being shuttled from one emergency foster home to another (the common occurrence) screamed out the results of such waiting. How long in the system does it take to become emotionally scarred and "unadoptable"? One professional, observing that babies are sometimes moved three or four times, asserted, "We know this is the classic way to raise a psychopath!" Studies in several states have shown that up to 70 percent of young people in the criminal justice system come from the foster care system. Wasn't it obvious that getting babies *out* was the first priority?

Yes, black families could give identity to black children. Yes, blacks on average adopted more than whites, for which they should be given great credit. Yes, obstacles should be removed from black adoption. But in the meantime those babies were in the hospitals having no one with whom to bond, which is as necessary to a child's emotional health as are food and water to physical life.

We remained painfully aware of the "blatant genocide" charges from black organizations. In reaction to that, the carnal side of me wanted to say, "Fine. Keep the baby. We're not doing this for *us.*" But that left the baby in its crib, and it wasn't his fault.

Fortunately, many black professionals "on the ground," having to deal with kids every day, knew that a hard line on this would doom individual children. The ones we worked with encouraged us to call various agencies and promised, "We'll help you find a baby. It doesn't matter where the baby comes from; there are so many that need your family."

We thought of Jesus' words, "Whoever welcomes one of these little children in my name welcomes me" (Mark 9:37). And we had the example of families in our church who had adopted black and biracial children.

Although we'd gone through the red tape of a private adoption and through all the foster care training, now we had to take eight weeks of adoption classes, fill out reams of questionnaires, do our homework, and get a black friend to send a letter vouching for our suitability. As I jammed these things into a busy schedule, I resented it. I thought, *If there's such a need, why do I have to jump through all these hoops again?* But as I prayed about it, I thought of missionaries taking the Good News into remote areas. Some worked through maddening red tape and numbing obstacles to help people who would just as soon kill them. Efforts to do good are seldom efficient or appreciated. If we were following God's direction, we couldn't expect him to drop every detail into our laps. Taking risks and perhaps being a fool were part of it, too.

Although we were licensed with DCFS and they were supportive, they were not finding an infant for us. So Jeanette put a call into a local Christian agency, Sunnyridge, and asked if they needed adoptive parents for black boys.

The response was immediately positive.

Six weeks later this fine agency invited us to an orientation meeting for those interested in cross-cultural adoption. We asked a staff member how many couples they had on their list waiting for babies. There were more than two hundred.

"How many are ready to adopt a black child?" we asked.

"At this time we have none," she said.

None? Not one couple? That confirmed to me that we were filling a vacuum instead of blocking someone else's opportunity.

Two days later a supervisor from DCFS called Jeanette. The judge had returned Kwame to his parents. Now it was official and final.

Jeanette, who had been on an emotional roller coaster of on-again, off-again signals, walked around the house, cried, and called a friend. In some ways it was a relief to know it was over. Yet—

Then something amazing happened, another one of those remarkable "coincidences." Just ten minutes after the call from DCFS, Sunnyridge called her.

"Could you transfer your license to our agency?"

"As of ten minutes ago, yes," Jeanette said.

"We have a healthy black boy born this morning in Chicago. We have no one for him."

Three days after that Todd, Greg, Rick, Jeanette, and I drove to Sunnyridge to get our new baby. Todd, still in high school but soon to leave for Marine Corps boot camp, wrote a paper about it which included this description:

We were let into a room in a huge house; against a wall was a bassinet. Inside lay the cutest four-day-old black baby. I walked over and picked up my new brother, held him in my arms and gazed into his pudgy face. His skin was so soft and his face adorable. I gave Joshua, the name we had decided on, to Greg to hold and we talked about how great it was to have a new brother. I noticed Rick looking out a window, walked over to him and asked him if he liked his new brother. "I love him!" he said. I laughed and gave him a big hug. We all went down the winding staircase with baby Joshua and said goodbye to the nice people we had met. We drove down the driveway full of smiles and excitement with our new, bigger family.

Warm sentiments from our tough marine.

When we arrived home, friends and neighbors came with presents and flowers and balloons and all their sincere support. And Joe Palma made another calligraphy: "Jesus Loves Joshua."

We went to Chicago to appear before a judge. In contrast to the impersonal bays, we found a courtroom actually friendly to children. Boxes with appropriate toys, families in the process of adoption, and in the inner chambers a judge in his upper eighties who just loved what he was doing and couldn't bear to retire.

As we stood before him, holding Josh, he pronounced some little homilies about how we should love and nurture this child. Yes, even in Chicago's court system one could experience a benediction.

Jeanette also experienced affirmation at O'Hare Airport. With Rick and baby Josh, she was checking her bags. A black skycap helping her with her luggage said, "Say, tell me something. What are you doing with these two boys?"

The question made Jeanette apprehensive. "We've adopted them," she said, studying his face. "What do you think about that?"

The skycap put his hand on Jeanette's arm. "Bless you. You know, if more people would do that, we wouldn't have such a problem with racism."

Exactly! How could it possibly not help break down walls if blacks and whites are blended in loving families?

Jeanette's destination that day was Pennsylvania. While there in a department store with Josh, a black stock boy stopped her. He asked in a cheerful way, "Is this baby yours?"

"Yes."

The young man wanted to know if she had adopted him.

"Yes, we have."

"That's wonderful!" he exclaimed. He asked about our family and then talked about his own family. He was very interested and very affirming.

It was a pattern. Whatever some professionals might think, whenever we would happen to meet African-Americans, they would show strong approval.

～

A little more than a month after Josh's birth was our twenty-fifth anniversary. Jeanette and I had talked about doing something very special to celebrate, maybe a weeklong trip. But the adoptions took priority, and we decided simply to go to a nearby resort for a day. Lois Badgero had said she'd baby-sit.

However, as we were snapping our suitcases shut and getting ready to haul Rick and Josh and all the kid gear into the car, we got a phone call. Lois was on the expressway with her two babies, and she apparently was experiencing a heart attack. She was on her way to the hospital.

Jeanette was given the name of the hospital, and when we arrived, Lois was having tests. Ray and Jeanette went in with her while I sat in the lobby with little Rick, Josh, and two "Badgero babies," ages six weeks and two weeks.

This was not quite what I'd anticipated for our anniversary. I'd wheel a stroller around some chairs, soothe a baby, answer Rick's questions, and wonder why God didn't seem to care if I got an ulcer. But as I hovered over the four little ones, I kept praying for Lois and her family.

It turned out that her problem was likely not an actual heart attack but a cardiac spasm. Her condition was serious but she would be okay.

So that evening instead of going to the resort, we went home with four little children. Jeanette was up during the night with the babies, and we tried to see humor in the situation and the foolishness of counting on plans. And what a better story we now have about our twenty-fifth than some "same old" travel tale of Hawaii or Austria.

Yet it was one more jarring instance of added pressures building up on us. Sure enough, we were starting a major addition to our house, with three new rooms and a bath. Back in foster training, when we heard Jane and Diane talking about their additions, we never thought it would happen to us.

I hoped we could soon get into normal rhythms. Adoptions and foster care were behind us. Rick had a sibling. We could go about raising these two boys along with our other children.

But then Jeanette had an experience which started some new wheels rolling.

A woman named Joanne, who knew that Jeanette had started an adoption support group, called often about black babies for whom she was trying to find homes. Jeanette networked with her and put her in contact with other families.

One day Joanne called with a special request. A family in Rockford was adopting a baby just born in Chicago. They had just had an adoption fall through and didn't want to see the baby till the mother signed the release papers. The family's lawyer wanted someone to pick up the baby and care for it for two days.

Would Jeanette drive to Presbyterian St. Luke's to get the baby?

Jeanette agreed, but she was as apprehensive as she was excited. It was nighttime, in the middle of winter, and she had never been to this hospital in downtown Chicago.

After driving the expressways, she entered the mother's room. The attractive black woman was in her mid-twenties. She and Jeanette went to the nursery, where the mother started to dress her very pretty baby girl. As she put on the baby's undershirt and sleeper, Jeanette felt sad for her. Was she thinking about never seeing her baby again? Was she asking herself, *Who is this stranger watching me dress my baby? Do I trust her? Am I doing the right thing, giving up my baby girl?*

The mother carried the baby as they rode the elevator to the lobby. Jeanette went out and got the car, then came back in to escort them. As they pushed through the big front doors and felt the chilly air, Jeanette had a sinking feeling. The mother had given birth just twenty-four hours before, and now Jeanette was taking the baby from her. She wondered if the mother would burst into tears or grab her baby and run.

After Jeanette opened the car door, the mother handed her the baby, and Jeanette gently secured her infant. The mother turned to start for the bus. "Can I drive you home?" Jeanette asked. "I'd be very happy to."

"No, no, that's all right," she insisted. "The bus is fine." Jeanette tried to persuade her, but the mother had made up her mind.

Jeanette watched her walk off in the snowy, cold night toward the bus stop. She felt terribly sad for her. What a contrast, Jeanette thought, to the way she herself had left the hospital with her own babies, with parents and flowers and a husband celebrating with her. This woman was going home all alone on a bus.

The infant slept in our house that night. However, two days later we got a call that the mother had changed her mind. She and a friend drove to our home to pick up her baby.

This experience gave Jeanette a strong empathy for birth mothers. It also started her thinking about our boys. Not too long after this Jeanette said to me as we were going to bed, "Wouldn't it be fun to have a little black girl in our home? Maybe it would be good for the boys—maybe they need a sister to grow up with. Someone to balance them out, to help them as black males."

I had an immediate response. "It's boys who are most endangered. Two little boys at my age is plenty. If God wants us to adopt a girl, then he needs to write a huge, clear message right across the sky."

chapter thirteen

*M*ichelle, Rick, Jeanette, and I drove the half hour from our house to Jean's place with our station wagon loaded with party supplies: salads, ham, rolls, condiments, pop, paper plates, a birthday cake, balloons, and presents. It was Rick's birth sister's birthday.

Jeanette had once asked Jean years before, "What are you going to do for Regina's birthday?" She said she wasn't going to do anything, so Jeanette started coordinating birthday celebrations for two of Rick's birth siblings, Regina and Mario, and for Jean herself.

However, I was always apprehensive coming here. Jean lived in a government-subsidized apartment complex, the parking spots full of old cars, many of them broken down. When we had first taken Rick as an infant, we had been told that ambulances wouldn't come here till two police cars had arrived first.

I parked in front of Jean's apartment and we all piled out. We grabbed full grocery bags and cake-size Tupperware containers and started toward the door. Regina was right there to meet us. A year older than Rick, she had been to our house and our church, and she loved to talk to us.

As we went back and forth carrying stuff in from the wagon, men who were grouped around a car across the street glanced over. At these parties I noticed it was always just women and children who came.

It was Regina's birthday, but the adults were as excited about the event as were the kids. Jean had invited friends, so about twenty were jammed into the small kitchen and living room. Jeanette presented Regina with a decorated, doll-shaped birthday cake she had made for her.

As the party progressed, I stepped outside to get some air and quietness. It seemed strange walking down the street under the gaze of children and men who probably saw me as an exotic intruder or an odd do-gooder.

At the end of the street was a playground. It had decent equipment, but no kids were on it at the moment. I smiled; maybe they were all at the party.

When I got back to the apartment, a boy about five was standing beside our station wagon, watching me. "Hi," I said. "How're you doing?"

He looked up at me and asked, "Are you that boy's daddy?"

He must have seen me holding Rick's hand or giving him something to carry. I looked at this little boy, so much like my son. Did he have a daddy? Did his daddy love him? What a different life from Rick's this boy was living.

"Yes, I'm his daddy."

I glanced over at the men standing around the car. Not that long ago each of them had been like this little boy. As they'd seen us trooping in with the bags of goodies, what had they thought? What was it like for them to live here where hardly any of them married, where there was always trouble around the corner and in the next house. For no good reason someone had recently shot Rick's father, Richard— not dead but plenty serious.

I looked at the little boy, soon to be a young man, and wondered what his life would be when he was twenty. What would I be like if I'd been born here? Would I be standing by one of those cars making small talk? Wondering every day what to do with myself?

Probably.

Yet sometimes the men did marry, and we were invited to one such happy occasion. Jean's best friend, Carol, was marrying the father of her four children. Jeanette had visited Carol's house several times, and we received an invitation.

The suburban church was a handsome brick building with a traditional sanctuary. When Jeanette and I arrived, we found Jean and the other bridesmaids very excited as they primped. Regina was carrying her new baby brother, Taron.

Jeanette, who loves newborns, went right to Regina and took Taron into her arms. It was obvious that although Jean had put Regina in charge of the month-old baby, Regina wanted very much to be part of the action and not tied down. So Jeanette volunteered to take care of him.

We stood around a long time before the wedding started, and then as it began, Jeanette whispered to me, "Can you hold Taron? Jean will want lots of pictures." I said okay and Jeanette started aiming her camera.

So there I sat with a new baby on my lap, and I thought about how ironic that was. A dozen years before, I had been sitting in our kitchen with Jeanette and a friend, who had said, "My mother always wanted a baby on her lap all the time. In fact, her dream was to have a new baby every year. Even when she had lots of work to do, nothing made her happier than to always have a baby on her lap."

I had sat across from this friend dumbfounded. A dream? Talk about my not being able to identify! To me, having so many babies around struck me as a nightmare, akin to one of Dante's punishments in a lower level of hell. Year after year after year doing all my work while having a baby on my lap?

After the woman left, I'd said to Jeanette, "Frankly, I can't imagine my doing that. A lifetime of babies on my lap? A nice quiet cell and a lifetime in jail would be preferable."

But here I was with a baby on my lap, and I managed to smile. He was cute and totally behaved all through the ceremony.

Afterward as we stood around, I held him as Jeanette kept taking photos. We felt comfortable with these black friends, but it struck me as a little weird. I was the only white guy at the wedding, and the only male hauling around a baby.

One Sunday my pastor asked how I was doing. "Frankly," I said, "I feel like a rabbit on the freeway."

I had read a study reporting on rabbits placed in a grassy divider between lanes on a freeway. The rabbits were given everything they needed: food, water, space. However, they had to live beside the constant traffic. Though nothing was life-threatening, the stress was catastrophic, with babies born dead and life spans dramatically shortened.

Just as the traffic stress had done deadly physical damage to the rabbits, so I felt my body reacting and my longing for peace intensifying. With the adoption process behind us, I was anxious to "normalize" our lives.

That's why it was so perplexing when it seemed that God indeed started to write across the sky about a newborn girl—writing in bold, strange script that confused us and mightily stretched our faith.

In February Jeanette received a phone call from a lawyer. A black professional couple in Chicago had a pregnant fifteen-year-old daughter almost ready to give birth. They had been searching for months all over Chicago for a black adoptive family but couldn't find one. Now they were desperate. The lawyer had told them about us—a white family with two black boys. The black couple had said, "Great!" and decided they wanted us to adopt their grandchild.

This news had come at a very pressured time. I felt, *Could God really be in this? Two is enough—and we have three birth kids. I'm a man desperate for solitude.* Yet might it be God's megaphone? These Chicago parents knew that if their grandchild went into the foster care system, it would be tragic.

"Isn't there anyone else?" I asked Jeanette. "You're the master networker. Find someone for these people."

She made calls all over the state but no one was available.

We were at that time racing on the fast track of preparing for the biggest event of my year: a week of board and staff meetings in Scottsdale, Arizona. Jeanette was to give leadership to spouse activities, so she was scurrying around getting baby-sitters and making all sorts of arrangements so she could come with me.

I fell into bed Thursday night, aware of this urgent request coming directly from the baby's family, but not enthusiastic about it. I didn't exactly want to take a baby on the plane to our board meetings, which was what would have to happen if everything worked out perfectly.

"It's very unlikely," Jeanette told me just before we went to sleep. "If it's not born tonight, this can't happen—the paperwork couldn't be completed on time. She's not scheduled to be induced until Saturday. We've told them we're open only to adopting a girl, and it could easily be a boy. We might as well forget about this."

That was fine with me. We seldom put out a specific fleece, but that night we prayed that if God wanted us to do this, the baby would be born that night and would be a girl.

The next morning I was at my office reading proofs of the letters section for the next issue of *Christianity Today*. We had run an article about children, and letter after letter talked about how children are a gift from the Lord, how they are incredibly valuable, how we must do more to welcome them into our lives. Without the slightest exaggeration, it was just as I was finishing the statements in these letters that the phone rang.

It was Jeanette. "The baby was born last night," she said, "and it's a healthy girl!"

I stared at the letters in front of me. I was dumbfounded. The timing of the call felt like huge, legible skywriting to me. What could I say? I told her I'd call her back. I then stepped into the next office and asked Paul Robbins to pray with me about it.

An hour later I told Jeanette I believed we should adopt this little girl. Jeanette's response was tears, relief, pleasure, and excitement.

That very morning, Friday, Jeanette and I had to fill out papers, get TB skin tests and updated medical forms and a copy of our marriage license. Since we didn't feel we could leave this newborn with a baby-sitter, we needed special permission to take her out of state. Then we drove into Chicago to sign more papers.

The black social worker, an older woman who obviously had seen it all, wished us well. "Go ahead and get your pink clothes. This seems like a done deal." I was surprised at how fast this train was moving. Jeanette was in contact with the parents of the new mother, and they were very positive about our adopting the baby.

As we drove back on the expressway discussing possible names, we felt as if we were in some sort of strange action movie. We decided on Lindsey. Lindsey Marie. On the way home we stopped at a children's store and bought a couple of baby girl outfits. Jeanette needed to collect enough baby items for a week in a hotel.

But then events in the Chicago hospital changed everything.

High school friends came to visit the fifteen-year-old mother. They told her in no uncertain terms that it would be a terrible thing to give up this baby. Heated discussions ensued, with the parents of the young mother extremely unhappy about all this advice their daughter was getting. They insisted that their daughter's baby be adopted, as she had agreed, and that they were not going to raise it for her. Certainly their daughter should not try to do so by herself.

In the midst of these arguments, a mother of one of the teenage friends said, "If your parents won't let you keep that baby, come to my house."

One can easily imagine how furious this must have made the new grandparents. They lashed out at the woman, creating another angry argument. However, they also saw how much the baby looked like their daughter, and they began to soften their stance. The baby went home with the mother and the adoption was off.

So there Jeanette and I were, our papers all signed, arrangements made to take this baby with us to Arizona, the skywriting from God observed and obeyed. The whole thing seemed terribly confusing. What was God up to, anyway? Was it him we were listening to, or were we making mere coincidences into signposts? Was it foolish to pay attention to such "signals from God"?

Over the next weeks we talked a great deal about the experience. It seemed evident that the journey of faith had more mystery and adventure than clarity. We seemed to be like explorers in a strange land, seeking wisdom from counselors, principles from Scripture, nudges from the Holy Spirit, but then having to make our interpretations and choose in the crossroads.

We concluded that perhaps God had burst into our lives to make us keep our door open. At the same time, we also concluded that at our age we shouldn't keep that door open forever. We prayerfully agreed to an open-door policy—from March through the summer. Michelle was getting married October 10. "Let's face it," I said, "September will be wedding chaos."

After September 1, we agreed, the door to further adoptions would be shut.

chapter fourteen

*T*hough now the door was open for a new Lindsey, we didn't have much time to think about it. Todd had completed his basic training in the Marine Corps, and we had to get him settled in college while he continued in the reserves. Jeanette, Michelle, Greg, and I had flown to San Diego to watch his graduation—a grand ceremony with a thousand marines in dress blues, cannons firing, military pageantry at its best.

We also were making wedding plans with Michelle's prospective in-laws. In May it was Michelle and fiancé Andy's college graduation near Boston. Then it was the summer, and nary a peep from an agency.

That seemed amazing in light of all the needs we'd been told about. But it was thoroughly okay by me. The summer was soon gone, and I felt I had my hands full with two little boys, birth kids, and lots of challenges at work.

Many small moments reinforced that we had made the right decision in adopting Josh and Rick. For instance, the time Rick, now six, got home after one of his connections with his birth family.

Jeanette had brought Regina to our house for the weekend. Just a year apart in age, she and Rick had typical brother-sister conflicts with lots of mutual put-downs. When Jeanette took Regina home with Rick tagging along, they found that Richard was in the apartment and asleep on the couch.

"Hi," Rick's birth father mumbled to him as he awoke and sat up. While Jeanette talked to Jean, he watched cartoons, pretty much ignoring Rick.

After Rick got home that evening, I started to put him to bed. Suddenly he grabbed me. He clung to me in a wrestling, humorous way and just kept at it, laughing, grabbing, horsing around. He obviously had tremendous skin hunger and this went on for about ten minutes.

Finally I held him by the shoulders and forced him to step back. He reached out his hands with open arms. "Daddy," he said, "I want you."

I asked, "For just a quiet hug, not a bunch of laughing?"

He nodded yes and came into my arms and hugged me tightly and affectionately for a long, long time. He obviously felt a lot of turmoil about where he actually fit, and he needed to reconnect with his dad.

The summer was soon gone and with it the thought of further adoptions. On September 10 I was in Colorado on business when Jeanette called. "Are you ready for this?" she asked.

"Probably not," I said cautiously.

"A little girl needs a home. She was born in Indiana."

I was standing in a strip mall with a pay phone on my ear, trying to absorb all this. "Well, have you called around? Girls are easier to place than boys." I stared at the parking lot and the assorted flow of humanity. "Surely there's somebody else who can take this child, some fine black family or some young, vigorous white one! We can't block someone else's opportunity. Isn't there anyone else?"

"No," Jeanette assured me. "I pressed them hard on that."

This was not the conversation I thought I'd be having.

"Jeanette, it's past the first of September. I thought we agreed that the door slammed shut that day. Otherwise how do we know this is something we should do?"

Her voice was perky as she answered, "But she was born on August 28!"

Well, just under the wire! What could I say?

Still, I'd grown wary of "coincidences." I promised only to think and pray about it.

I was with my wise colleague Paul Robbins, and we decided to drive out to the Broadmoor Hotel to walk around.

The year had been stressful on all fronts, and I was showing signs of depression: exhaustion, stomach pains, loss of emotions. Whatever it was that stress released into the bloodstream, it was certainly doing a number on my body. To think of another baby in our noisy, multifaceted family felt like a very large, weighty straw on the camel's back. Part of me felt excited about having another daughter, but another part felt it was just plain crazy.

As we walked around the lake at the hotel, I admitted to Paul that I had more than once thought about how good it would be to someday snuggle down into my "cozy, green grave"—to quietly die—and to leave the pressures and troubles to others.

What were my responsibilities before God? To the boys I had already adopted? To my colleagues at *Christianity Today*? To my family and to myself?

We walked around the lake many times, trying to discern God's will. I knew that the Lord worked in mysterious ways. I had long ago concluded that our involvement with the children had been all tied up with his purposes. In fact, the past years had all seemed remarkably full of "God's surprises."

But I was going down hard on this one. My body and my emotions urged great caution.

On the plane coming back I opened my New Testament to Luke's gospel. I figured the kind, wise physician might counsel restraint. I was particularly thinking about Jesus' words about not building a tower or starting a war until you've counted the cost. It seemed to me that I should be counting the cost, especially considering I'd be about seventy when this newborn girl would be getting out of high school. Would we have the resources and energies?

Well, what might Luke tell me?

What first struck a chord was Mary's being "greatly troubled" by the angel come to announce that, though a young virgin, she would have a baby. But when the angel said, "The Holy Spirit will come upon you, and the power of the Most High will overshadow you," her response was, "I am the Lord's servant. May it be to me as you have said" (1:26–38).

Mary visited her cousin Elizabeth, who was filled with the Holy Spirit. Elizabeth said that Mary's child was blessed and that as soon as she'd heard Mary's voice, her own baby in her womb had "leaped for joy" (1:39–45).

Then Mary magnificently praised God, saying, "The Mighty One has done great things for me—holy is his name" (1:46–56).

There it was, right in the beginning of Luke: the joy of children. Not a direct application to my situation but clear about the impact of obedience and about the fact that children bring joy as well as responsibility.

I kept reading the gospel of Luke and marked these words from Jesus:

> "Give to everyone who asks you, and if anyone takes what belongs to you, do not demand it back. Do to others as you would have them do to you" (6:30–31).

> "If you love those who love you, what credit is that to you? Even 'sinners' love those who love them" (6:32).

> "From everyone who has been given much, much will be demanded" (12:48).

Having just been walking around the luxurious Broadmoor and now jetting in comfort to a city with so many desperate children, this seemed a stern statement.

Then I read these words from Jesus: "When you give a luncheon or dinner, do not invite your friends, your brothers or relatives, or your rich neighbors. . . . Invite the poor, the crippled, the lame, the blind, and you will be blessed" (14:12–14).

I was looking for caution and all I found was challenge. And when I finally arrived at Jesus' words about building a tower, I was completely surprised at what it actually said. I had been fuzzily thinking that the point was, Don't be stupid and overextend yourself. But that wasn't the point at all. In fact, it was exactly the opposite.

It's in chapter 14. Jesus first says that love and obedience to him must be far, far greater than one's love for one's own family. Then he says, "And anyone who does not carry his cross and follow me cannot be my disciple. Suppose one of you wants to build a tower. Will he not first sit down and estimate the cost to see if he has enough money to complete it?" (14:27–28).

I had been remembering that verse as urging caution in making commitments.

Jesus then describes a king about to go to war. "Will he not first sit down and consider whether he is able with ten thousand men to oppose the one coming against him with twenty thousand?" (14:31).

Again, I had thought that the point was, Don't start something you can't finish. Like adopt a child when you're too old.

But Jesus drives home an entirely different point. "In the same way, any of you who does not give up everything he has cannot be my disciple" (v. 33).

Neither Luke nor Jesus gave me cause for caution. If anything, the whole life of Jesus as recorded by Luke seemed to be a life of throwing caution to the wind.

My plane landed at O'Hare. By the time I got home, it was too late to talk much about the decision we'd have to make the next day.

Very early the next morning at the office, I opened my Bible. Wouldn't you know that it opened to this statement in Job: "Man is born to trouble as surely as sparks fly upward" (5:7).

I agreed with that!

And this from Job: "My groans pour out like water. What I feared has come upon me" (3:24–25).

I thought, *True!* In contrast, Jeanette had told me that the verse she'd found on the weekend was one in Hebrews about Abraham's joy in his son. But here I was getting jerked back and forth again, opening my Bible this decisive morning to Job cursing the day of his birth.

I turned to Proverbs, knowing there were lots of verses there relating to wisdom and caution. But chapter after chapter all I saw were admonitions to care for the poor and needy and to reach out to orphans.

Jeanette and I are not the sort who simply poke around Scripture and take things out of context. I thought of the overall thrust of Proverbs and Job. Job had been jerked around, never being told what God was up to. That seemed similar to the way God had dramatically crashed into our lives with that urgent call about the child soon to be born in Chicago.

Job, despite all this, simply said, "Though he slay me, yet will I hope in him" (13:15). And at the end he proclaims to God, "No plan of yours can be thwarted" (42:2).

I realized that in Jeanette's and my lives, no plan of God's could be thwarted. And ultimately all of Scripture spoke with one consistent voice. Proverbs said it: "Many are the plans in a man's heart, but it is the LORD's purpose that prevails" (19:21).

I lingered on that last chapter of Job. "The LORD blessed the latter part of Job's life more than the first. . . . Nowhere in all the land were there found women as beautiful as Job's daughters, and their father granted them an inheritance along with their brothers" (42:12, 15).

I had no idea if this little girl in Indiana was beautiful or not. But physical beauty was irrelevant—the beauty of spirit that we might give as an inheritance to her and to her brothers was eternally important.

Finally I read, "After this, Job lived a hundred and forty years; he saw his children and their children to the fourth generation. And so he died, old and full of years" (42:16).

I certainly didn't claim as a promise that I'd live another hundred and forty years. But at fifty-three, the Lord just might give me another twenty.

Life is full of risks, and in faith we make our judgments as best we can. I called Jeanette and told her I thought we should go ahead with the adoption.

Somehow, making the phone call and the decision released energies within me. I had formed a conviction that this was what we should do, that I should give myself to this little unknown girl and to Josh and Rick, and that all of my responsibilities were in God's hands. And from that came a spiritual shift that lessened the sense of stress that had been accumulating for so long.

I sensed that this power of the Holy Spirit had come from obedience. Jesus said he had come that we might have joy, but he forever was commanding us to recklessly give ourselves away. The two seemed to go together in a tragic, suffering world.

One week before Michelle's wedding, Lindsey entered our home. And in no time at all the wedding day arrived.

Just before the ceremony, I stepped into the church and descended the stairs to the lower level. Somewhere in one of these rooms, Michelle was dressing for the big moment.

Up until one week ago Michelle had been my only daughter. And I would never have words to describe all she meant to me. A few months before, while filling out a form for Sunnyridge, I had tried to express how I as a father would relate to a new daughter.

I had gotten teary-eyed as I wrote, for I said things like a father and daughter are a wonder under the sun, that a dad and his little girl have a special magic. I said a daughter is a princess whom a father always, always loves. . . . "That's just the way it is at our house."

Lindsey's birth mother, a young college student, presumably read my words before saying yes to our adopting her little girl. What had gone through her mind? Would she have seen mental pictures of a white father holding her little princess? Would that have reassured her? How delightful if she could have known that her little girl not only was in my arms on this special day but would be hugged by everyone, including the bride.

And here I was in the lower level of the church, about to see Michelle emerge among her bridesmaids. Suddenly there she was with her radiant smile, and all the years of magic between us drew her into my arms. I kissed her cheek. What a beautiful woman! What a privilege to be a father!

All eight grandparents had earlier celebrated their fiftieth wedding anniversaries—a grand heritage for Michelle and Andy. And now about two dozen Gordon College students had come from Boston, full of faith and camaraderie, music and laughter. A churchful of relatives and friends.

Soon Michelle was on my arm, walking down the aisle, flower petals beneath our feet. Then I was "giving her away" to Andy.

The wedding was an ethnic mixture. African-American Rick as ring bearer in his tux, looking classy and confident. Half our kids white, half black. Nigerian-American Karba sitting with her newborn boy on her lap. My Norwegian cousin Hjordis and husband Johan, with Hjordis dressed in the exquisite Stavanger costume she had made. Andy's uncle and grandfather playing Scottish bagpipes as Michelle and Andy were introduced as Mr. and Mrs. and walked down the aisle.

A few months before, at Michelle and Andy's graduation from Gordon College, James Earl Mundia, Anglican bishop from Kenya, attended the ceremony of his son's graduation. After receiving an honorary doctorate, the bishop asked a professor to join him at the podium. He gripped the professor's white hand, intertwining their fingers. Then he held both hands aloft, declaring that white and black fingers are like white and black piano keys, which—together—can make wonderful music!

A short time after hearing that, we went to McDonald's with our young black children and older white children. Across from us sat a middle-aged black couple with two little white boys they were caring for.

Blacks caring for whites. Whites for blacks. Beautiful music together. Each heritage celebrated. Respect and love going beyond family and race.

Alan Paton, author of *Cry, the Beloved Country* and a heroic spokesman for black rights in South Africa during apartheid, prayed that others could be used as God's instruments "in the never-ending work of healing and redemption." He believed that "only as such instruments can the Christian encounter hatred, injury, despair, and sadness...by throwing off his helplessness and allowing himself to be made the bearer of love."

In the joy of the wedding, I prayed that our family would be such sowers of God's peace. Four sons: two white, two black. A blond daughter, a black daughter. A new son-in-law.

Michelle, radiant and beautiful, moving among throngs of well-wishers, starting her new life. Lindsey, a tiny sleeping bundle in my arms, a new Myra about to love and bond with our family. She would create once more the wonder of father and daughter and amaze us all that God would so marvelously bring her into our lives.

And soon Joe Palma created a final calligraphy: "Jesus Loves Lindsey."

chapter fifteen

*O*ne of the joys of Michelle's wedding and Lindsey's adoption was our parents' good health and enthusiastic support. Though at their age they couldn't baby-sit for us, they were cheerleaders and showed all their grandchildren lots of love.

But three years after the wedding, the health picture had changed. Both Jeanette's dad in Wisconsin and my mother in Pennsylvania had been diagnosed with terminal cancer. Through the fall our family was on a double deathwatch. Brain surgery for Mom, with Jeanette flying to my parents' home and nursing her for weeks while I cared for the kids; my flying to see Mom in the hospital; Jeanette driving to Wisconsin to be with her dad. Pressures of trying to get childcare, keeping up with the office, dealing with all the emotions.

But now in mid December it was nearly over. Two weeks before, Jeanette's wonderful father had died. With our six children and extended families we had grieved at his funeral. Now Mom too was near the end.

I awakened in "my room" in my parents' Pennsylvania home. Downstairs I heard Dad in the kitchen making the oat bran. This morning, unlike countless mornings, Mom wouldn't join him for their traditional breakfast. She was in a coma on a hospital bed in the living room.

In the kitchen Dad was ready to pour the steaming oat bran into shallow bowls, ones familiar from my boyhood. I hugged him; then he poured the hot cereal. He and Mom had always sprinkled Millers Bran and wheat germ on top, so I followed suit.

"Has she said anything?" I asked. Dad had slept on the rollaway by her, as he had every night since hospice brought the bed.

"No, not a sound except for her breathing."

After breakfast I stepped into the living room. It was painful to see how emaciated she was. Mom did not look alive at all.

"Good morning, Mom."

No response. Except for her breathing, she seemed already gone. It seemed strange talking to this form on the bed, which was barely reminiscent of my living mother. Next to the windows was the big table where she had so often hosted crowds of relatives and friends. On the nightstand was the lamp Richie had made on a lathe in school. She who had so compassionately and faithfully stood by so many children and hurting people was leaving us forever.

I touched her shoulder, her arm, her hand. *Does she feel my touch? I wondered. Can she hear me?*

"Mom, it's a beautiful morning outside. There's a light blanket of snow out there, sparkling on the trees and lawn. I know how much you love to look at the mountain, and it's all white against the blue sky."

I kept describing the scene outside but I felt a little foolish. There was no sign of comprehension. Yet people say you should talk to a comatose person as if he or she can hear. "Mother," I said, "can you hear the birds outside? I know how you love them. I wish you could see them. Do you hear me? Are you hearing me, Mom? I love you very much."

And then, although no other part of her body moved, the muscles in her jaw tightened and stretched. It was as if she were willing her muscles to move with her old implacable will—as if she were coming up from death itself. Her thin face on the pillow was as motionless as a statue, but with a supreme effort she forced her skeletal jaw and cheeks slowly, slowly up into what was unmistakably a smile.

"Mom, I see your smile!" I exclaimed. "I see your smile! I know you are hearing me." I paused a moment, then said, "Mother, thank you for that wonderful gift."

I kept talking to her, resolving from then on to keep her in the conversation whenever possible, even if she did seem already gone. In the kitchen Dad was washing dishes. I called in to him and told him about her smile. "That's good," he said simply, and he too smiled at me.

I took a walk out on the mountain trails I'd loved for more than forty years. In my mind was the image from just a few months ago of the moment my mother had beckoned to me and then given me a long, long hug. Thoughts of that hug lingered as I walked. She had never before held me so tightly and so long. Then she did the same with Johnny, who later said, "She was saying good-bye to us."

My eyes filled with tears as I walked past hickory, oak, and aspen. Death is such a surreal intruder.

I thought of some years ago sitting across the kitchen table from Mom when she was not all that much older than I am now. She said, "You know, you just about learn how to live... and then it's time to go."

She had described her first experience of realizing she was "old." Some boys were playing by the water, and one of them said, "Why don't you go ask that old lady over there?" Mom had wondered who the boy was talking about. What old lady? Then she finally realized, "The boy was talking about *me!*"

How quickly we lose our youth. I thought of the wedding pictures of my handsome parents, who had honeymooned in Washington, D.C. Photos of Dad and Mom dating, leaning on a snazzy convertible. Young, vigorous—but now old and frail.

Life is not only brief, I thought, climbing along a ridge edged by stones that farmers had tossed there a century ago, *but tragic.* And not only the Richies from dysfunctional families but also people from stable immigrant Norwegian families experience the dark threads in life's tapestry. My dad lost both his parents before getting engaged to my mother. Mom's parents, not long after arriving in America, had a baby, Lydia. The child died. They had another baby girl and named her Lydia also, but she too died before she was a year old.

They named their third girl Esther—my mother—and then they had my Uncle Dave. His daughter, my beautiful cousin Lois, was killed at age twenty-one in a car crash. Her brother, David, later lost his wife Elsbeth to leukemia. My brother, Johnny, experienced divorce after seventeen years of marriage and three children.

We are all part of the brokenness, and Mother had always tried to heal some of that brokenness wherever she turned. Always she was expressing gratitude for God's blessings and his creation. As I walked these trails, it didn't seem at all possible that I would get back and enter that house and not find her there with hot soup or an encouraging word.

Next day there was no change in Mom's condition. She had made no movement of any kind since her smile. I moistened her mouth with one of the little sponge devices from hospice, which is like a toothbrush. On the couch the colorful afghan she had made reminded me of the afghans she'd knitted for Rick and Josh and Lindsey, each made of the colors they chose, each carried often around the house and at night laid across each bed.

The form on this bed seemed so absent from me, so unlike my mother.

But I talked to her anyway. "Mom, you have been an absolutely wonderful mother to me. You've encouraged me every step of the way." Although I had told her these things many times before, I so longed for her to know deep down in these last moments how precious she was to me. Yet her body showed no response.

"You know, from the time I was a little boy, you have been my soul mate. I remember sitting with you in Grandmom's house when I was very small, both of us getting warm over the grate, talking about school and my reciting poems, and agreeing together how fortunate we were. Mom, I love you very much. I always, always will."

I was speaking to a motionless stick figure. No smile was forthcoming, and I doubted she had heard what I'd been saying.

But then I saw something below her eye. The skin looked wet. And then I realized a large tear was forming. It pooled at the edge of her eye, then suddenly spilled over and ran down her cheek in a long, wet line.

I was stunned. I was exuberant. I felt tears forming in my own eyes. "Thank you, Mother," I said. "I see your tears. You've heard me. I wish we could go back and relive some of those good, warm days fifty years ago. You were wonderful to me, and you will always be in my thoughts. Always!"

That night was Mom and Dad's sixtieth anniversary. Johnny and his wife, Donna, came over and with Dad and me celebrated their remarkable six decades together. Mom remained in her coma; perhaps she heard us celebrating and telling her how much we loved her. We hoped so.

The next morning Dad called to me from the bottom of the stairs. "Harold, you'd better check on your mother."

I came down and stepped into the room. She looked the same as she had the past week, but now she was no longer breathing. I put my hand on hers.

Walking in the woods earlier, I'd seen a tree split right down the middle so that the earth at its base was heaved up. It was a tearing asunder, like Mother torn irrevocably from me. All my driving engines of career and service to God, my respect and love for Jeanette, my openness to foster children—to embrace Kwame and to adopt Rick, Josh, and Lindsey—all this had at their core the unshakable commitments and love of the woman who had just left this room.

Now all of the challenges were passed on to me.

When C. S. Lewis's wife, Joy, died, he said of her that she had been both "my daughter and my mother" as well as "mistress" and "friend." Joy had been all that any male friend had ever been to him.

So with my mother. Time passes and all the roles shift and take new shapes. Son and mother. Father and children. Time inexorably turning the pages.

As I stood there, boyhood scenes appeared in my mind: Mom's warming my nearly frostbitten hands in the kitchen; her praising a school paper; her responding to my questions by saying that as an ant can't understand our ways, neither can we understand God's. These blended with scenes of my comforting Todd after an ugly schoolyard incident, of Michelle's little fingers locked unyieldingly on my neck at bedtime, of Greg's preschool questions about when God began. Now my birth children have grown beyond all that—as I did—and it's Rick with the schoolyard troubles; it's Josh with the locked arms on my neck, hanging in the air and refusing to let go; it's Lindsey with wide-eyed questions.

Mother was at the center of all these interlocking scenes. She always would be. Male, female. Old, young. Mother, son. Father, children. All our moments and identities intertwined and significant.

My soul friendship with my mother was forever altered. Yet it also had not changed at all.

chapter sixteen

*J*eanette, Rick, and I sat in our station wagon, waiting in a department store parking lot in the north side of Chicago. I was nervous about this clandestine rendezvous.

"Rick, do you see anything?"

"No."

Rick was nine now and eager to catch sight of Kwame. It had been four years since any of us had seen him. We all stared at the big wooden fence separating the stores from the apartments where Kwame and his family lived.

"Just watch," Jeanette said. "They'll come around that corner." She wasn't uneasy like me, just wanting to see the boy she had loved so deeply. She and Anna had talked by phone. Since Walter was there only sporadically, Anna had suggested that we visit Kwame. But just in case Walter stopped by, we were to meet in this parking lot.

"They're late," I said. "I'm still not sure this is a good idea."

"They'll come," Jeanette said, "and it will be fine. Anna said Walter's hardly ever around anymore."

Rick saw them first. From behind the fence Anna appeared with four well-dressed little boys in tow. Kwame was now seven. We drove closer to them; they all piled into our wagon, and then we took off toward a nearby McDonald's.

We spread out across two tables with our cheeseburgers, fries, drinks, and lots of crayons and coloring books. The boys were quiet; Rick was beside Kwame. Jeanette and I had said only hi to him—no hugs, no extravagant displays of emotion. We feared creating problems by showing special attention to Kwame, so we treated all the boys equally, like neighbor kids. But as we talked, every time Jeanette's eyes would lock on Kwame's, he would give her a big smile.

Kwame not only remembered us, he had some very good memories. Anna felt differently from Kwame's dad about how we had nurtured her son, and she had told Jeanette on the phone, "He remembers being in your house. He remembers going to Bible study with you and learning about God." We had worried a great deal that the father's poisoning him against us would cause Kwame not only to reject us but to reject God and distort the boy's sense of identity. But apparently Kwame was sorting it out, because Anna had asked Jeanette, "Do you know what Kwame said to me once?"

"No, what?"

"Kwame said, 'I had a good childhood, you know, Mom.'"

That blew us away. He was referring to his three years with us, and when we heard those words, they resonated in our souls, not for our sakes but for Kwame's. If he believed that, then he could emotionally and spiritually put his two worlds together.

When we dropped the boys off back at the parking lot, we felt very hopeful for Kwame.

Two years later we were again waiting for Kwame, this time with Rick and also Josh and Lindsey. But it wasn't to be a joyous reunion. We were in a funeral home talking to Kwame's relatives. His grandmother, Anna's mother, had always been very friendly to us, and she had called Jeanette with tragic news. "I knew you would want to know. The boys couldn't wake their mother this morning."

Anna was less than forty, but she had died in her bed from an apparent asthma attack.

Anna dead. What a blow to her little family!

We thought Anna's mother was bringing Kwame, but when she arrived at the funeral home, she didn't have him with her. "Oh, he'll be here soon," she said. "They're just out buying funeral clothes for him."

In some ways Anna's mother was in the same boat as Jeanette and me. As Walter had tried to poison the boys and Anna against us, he did the same against Anna's mother.

Jeanette anxiously watched every car that pulled up. We didn't know how the boys were going to react. When Jeanette saw Kwame get out of the car with his brothers, she went right over and gave him a big hug as he entered the funeral home. But Kwame seemed shy and reserved.

Now he was nine, far taller than when we'd met him at McDonald's. After the hug he stood there awkwardly. What was going through his mind? What were we now to him? He didn't look at me, but I stepped closer to him and reached out to hug him. I thought about how he used to leap into my arms and how he would laugh, his eyes lighting up above a clever expression on his mouth.

Now all that was barely a memory for him. Kwame's hug was wooden, his face impassive. He had lost us and now his mother. How would he handle all this?

We were impressed with Anna's family, sensing stability. No one had anything good to say about Walter, and when Jeanette asked if he might come to the funeral, they said—as if glad of it—"No, he won't be here. We don't know where he is."

Anna's best friend, an energetic and thoughtful woman, knew right away who we were. "Oh, yes, Anna talked about you a lot."

But now Anna was gone. How difficult it was to square the boys' loss with the message that God is love.

God is love—how could this be, in this funeral home in Chicago, in all this city's suffering?

I thought of Oswald Chambers' realism when he admitted that it's far from evident that God is love. In fact, it looks as if it's the exact opposite. Yet as we turn to God, we experience his love. And we are called to be active instruments of his love.

The question on everyone's mind was, Who will take care of Kwame and his brothers? We were told that their eldest brother, now twenty-three, had volunteered. Handsome, cool, he had a very pleasant way about him. He was living with a young Hispanic woman who had borne his child. This was the same young man who as a teenager had helped Jeanette carry all that furniture upstairs to Anna's apartment.

We enjoyed talking to him, but I wondered what his sources of income would be, besides Social Security for the boys. I wished all the best for all of them. As we left, he said firmly, "Call anytime you want."

Jeanette always sent Christmas cards to Anna's mother, who often said Kwame should be able to see us. So when he was at her home during the Christmas holidays, she had him call. Jeanette invited him and his brothers to come for New Year's Day.

Greg, home from college, was apprehensive about his coming; the wounds were still painful. In contrast, Rick was enthusiastic about having his old playmate in the house.

Bright and early on New Year's, Jeanette drove into Chicago and picked them up. As Kwame with his brothers walked in our front door for the first time in nearly seven years, he seemed at ease, his eyes alert and probing. Rick, Josh, and Lindsey mixed easily with the four boys. Despite his misgivings, Greg pitched right in and helped as we bundled up to go sledding.

When the boys got back wet, happy, and hungry, we put out tacos and mugs of hot chocolate and soon had a lively crowd around the kitchen table. The boys were consistently polite, eager, and full of fun.

After the meal Kwame was looking at our bulletin board with its dozens of family photos. Jeanette came up to him and asked, "Would you like to see photos of you as a little boy?"

"Yes."

She led him to the living room, where he and his brothers then sat on the couch looking at the photo album Jeanette had long ago made of his three years with us. Kwame was very interested! There he was with Michelle, Todd, Greg, Rick, or standing with a neighbor at their picnic or riding a trike on the sidewalk. He remembered many things about the family, and the photos brought it all back to life.

When it was time to go, we each hugged Kwame, and he warmly hugged us back. When Jeanette and Greg loaded the boys into the wagon to take them back to the city, I felt a sense of completion. As I tucked Josh and Lindsey in for the night, I thought about how much is out of our hands and how often we must simply pray and look to God to be at work in his own way and time.

When I first began to write this book, I found my old notes describing my dream about Kwame. The notes made me relive the dream, with all its complexities and tears. Once again I was seeing Kwame walking up to me, saying in a strange voice, "They want to know if I can stay with you". . . and the children gathering around us with gaily painted faces contrasting with Kwame's blank stare. As I read, once again I felt the helplessness of being a human father.

Moments after reading the notes about the dream, I "coincidentally" turned to an article by Henri Nouwen in *Leadership* journal. It spoke with simple yet magnificent power to what I was feeling, for it spoke of Christ and his heavenly Father.

With a mental image of Kwame's face larger than life, I read, "To pray is to listen to the One who calls you 'my beloved daughter,' 'my beloved son.' To pray is to let that voice speak to the center of your being, to your guts, and to let that voice resound in your whole being."

Would Kwame ever experience this sort of prayer? To know deep in his guts that he was the beloved son of the heavenly Father?

I thought of all my children—adopted, birth, foster—all born into an unforgiving world. I thought of how Michelle painting the children's faces with colors and joy was like the Holy Spirit bringing healing and bright life. But before the colors in my dream could enliven Kwame's face, I had awakened to reality.

Reality. What was it?

Nouwen said this about every adult, every child: "Who am I? I am the beloved. That's the voice Jesus heard when he came out of the Jordan River: 'You are my beloved; on you my favor rests.' And Jesus says to you and to me that we are loved as he is loved. That same voice is there for you."

All of us born for the Father's love. That resonated. God loved Kwame and his brothers even more than we did.

chapter seventeen

*I*n the junior high auditorium, little girls and boys in rows of folding chairs fumble with their costumes. It is the dance performance class's big moment—the spring performance. Parents drape coats and paraphernalia over the seats. I grip Jeanette's cameras on the empty seat beside me, my eyes tracking Lindsey and her little friend Beth across the aisle.

The children are turned out in remarkable costumes. Lindsey is a bright yellow-and-black bumblebee.

And I am a shut-down zombie.

I should feel wonderful at my daughter's big moment. I want to. But somehow publishing stress at work and pressures at home have combined to shut down my system, like switching off a computer. It feels as if deep within my psyche the entire structure of weight-bearing supports has suddenly been knocked away and the system has collapsed.

Lindsey rushes up. "I need Mommy."

"She'll be here soon."

"I need Mommy *now*," she says urgently.

Off the bumblebee buzzes. I am amazed at how my stress reaction is like getting walloped by the flu. The very same symptoms—dead-tired, no emotions, everything a burden. But unlike the flu, since it is "only stress," I had to show up here instead of falling into bed.

My eyes see costumed children dancing, but my mind keeps trying to figure out why my system has shut down. I think about an article I read on the effects of stress on POWs after World War II. Apparently the trauma of being taken prisoner and expecting the worst messed up their bodies' "fight or flight" mechanisms. Contrasted with a control group of similar men, the POWs experienced over the next fifty years *four times* the cardiac troubles and fatal heart attacks.

Maybe that's what happened to me, I think. *A valve has gotten stuck open and won't stop pouring chemicals into my blood. I can't just "get a grip"; I can't just "snap out of it."*

Yet I also think, *So I'm overstressed. Who isn't? Other men my age who have adopted black children have endured much more. Ray Badgero was diagnosed with advanced cancer, beat it, and adopted two more! And our wives have carried incredible loads.*

But I also dredge up the memory of a friend who battled the outrageous court system to adopt two black boys. Then he suffered a heart attack. And I can't help but think, *It killed him! All that stress. He literally gave his life for those boys.*

Then again, who knows? Maybe adoption stress wasn't it at all. Maybe hugs from the boys gave him an extra year of life.

Jeanette arrives and my grim expression adds to her burdens. She aims her cameras, deals with Lindsey's sudden refusal to perform, gets group shots afterward. I gather up coats and equipment.

At home I tell Jeanette that my stress reaction is like the flu, that I'm not trying to be a spoilsport. I tell her about World War II POWs. She listens—quietly.

I say to her, "Guy after guy my age has told me, 'I couldn't stand to do what you're doing. It would just be impossible.' But my response is that I feel exactly the same way. It's impossible for me too!"

Jeanette listens, busily sorting laundry as I go on. "Men younger than I am say they love their grandchildren, but they can't take more than one day at a time with them. One guy spent just three days with his grandchildren, then said, 'Of all the sights in the entire world, there is none more beautiful than the receding taillights of the van taking your grandchildren home.'"

Jeanette frowns. She does not like this talk, thinks it's foolish. But I tell her a supposedly humorous version anyway. "A woman and her husband are saying good-bye to their grandchildren loaded in the van. As everyone is waving, the van accidentally runs over her foot. Turning her head so no one can see her intense pain, she says to her husband, 'Keep waving! Keep waving!'"

Jeanette doesn't smile at the joke. She's struggling with her own feelings of stress—three little kids, three older kids, demands from every direction. "I don't like that story. Sure, you can think like that— but I'm just not going to!"

"Well," I said, "it helps me to know that people our age don't find it easy."

"Of course they don't! But we've made the decision about the kids. I'm afraid to let myself think like that. What are we going to do— send them back?"

I retreat to my den, sit down heavily, and turn to my friend Fénelon, the French Christian who lived in the late 1600s. On the very first page of his book *The Seeking Heart* he tells me, "Do not resist what God brings into your life. Be willing to suffer. God prepares a cross for you that you must embrace without thought of self-preservation."

Ouch! Beside those words I had written some months before, "Adoptions!" and then an arrow to this: "See God's hand in the circumstances of your life. . . . Nothing so shortens and soothes your pain as the spirit of nonresistance to your Lord. Do not reject the full work that the power of the Cross could accomplish in you."

A few pages later I had marked: "Bear your cross. Learn to see yourself as you are, and accept your weakness until it pleases God to heal you."

And then I read for probably the fiftieth time the words that had emblazoned themselves on my mind: "Embrace the difficult circumstances you find yourself in—even when you feel they will overwhelm you. Allow God to mold you through the events he allows to enter your life. The events of life are like a furnace for the heart."

Fortunately, the children injected lots of laughter, the ideal antidote to stress. For instance, I laughed heartily when Josh asked out of the blue, "Daddy, do killer whales burp?"

Our friends the Badgeros adopted a baby girl name Mercy. Josh loves babies, and before Mercy was a year old, he decided he would marry her when they grew up. From then on he was making all sorts of judicious plans, such as, "When I grow up with Mercy, I'm going to let her have a minivan, and I'm going to have a red Suburban."

Josh has a terrific smile, another good antidote to stress. At the Y, instructors told Jeanette, "Josh is always smiling. Even when he's under the water, he's smiling." Josh has always been fearless. At two he'd jump into the deep end of the pool, sink to the bottom, come up coughing as if half drowned, then get up on the edge and jump in again.

One Sunday morning at breakfast, dog-lover Josh said, referring to the neighbor's boxer, "I really like Sherman."

Lindsey put down her spoon and said, "He likes Sherman more than Jesus."

"No," Josh instantly lectured back like a seminary student. "I just like Sherman."

Later Lindsey told me we needed a new refrigerator.

"Why?" I asked.

"Because there's lots of marbles, rings, and spiderwebs under it."

When Lindsey was learning about her adoption, she looked at me intently, as if to help me grasp a complex situation, and slowly enunciated, "Your wife is not my mother." She started early with her questions. Barely three, she asked, "When we go to heaven, will I have brown skin?"

"I don't know," I said. "Maybe I'll have brown skin and you'll have white skin."

She broke into a huge smile. "Goody!"

"Don't you like having brown skin?" I asked. "I think it's beautiful."

"No. White skin is more gooder."

So even at that age she had come to that sad conclusion. "In heaven," she later told me, "you and Mom be brown and I'll be brown. You be white and Mommy be white and I'll be white." Once she said very cheerfully, as if full of important new information, "You're not my daddy. My daddy is brown. You're white."

Later she wanted to know what color God was. "White like you, right?" she said soberly.

"No," I answered. "Actually, when Jesus was on earth, he lived in the Mid-east and probably had brown skin like yours."

"Oh," she said.

Lindsey brought up skin color a lot. A lighthearted book about it we loved to read together was titled *You Be Me, I'll Be You.* "It's about me and Daddy," she told friends.

In the book, little Anna is sad because she thinks she's not pretty. She doesn't like the brown color of her face, hands, or arms. "I want to be like you," she says.

"How silly," says her white father, who would "do anything not to have such a pale face."

But she wants to have head and hair like his. "Suppose we trade heads?" her father suggests.

And they do. Anna helps him smear coffee grounds all over his face, and she braids his hair. He puts flour on Anna's face, and she puts his hat on her head.

Then they go off to meet Mom in town, his hair looking like tree branches in a storm, both very silly. Passersby smile. A child asks if there's a circus in town. Mom, on seeing them, puts hands on hips, indulgently calls them clowns, and says, smiling, that they need a shower.

Among other things, it's a stress-busting book. And if we hadn't adopted Rick, Josh, and Lindsey, a melancholy Norwegian like me wouldn't be reading it.

God's ways truly are mysterious. All we can do in life is embrace what God puts into our arms. Here is Lindsey, the girl we almost didn't get, who not only loves me intensely but says so often. God crash-landed her into our lives when I thought I was at the end of my capacities, this amazing girl who plies me with questions and serious talk and laughter, all as if she were perfectly designed to be my daughter.

Fénelon summed it up pretty well: "Don't worry about the future—worry quenches the work of grace within you. When God gives you comfort, enjoy it. I want you to realize how continually you will feel suspended in the air and not allowed to walk on solid ground. The comfort you find in this moment will be completely inadequate for the next. Let God act in your life in whatever way He chooses. All you must do is be faithful to what He asks of you."

chapter eighteen

*F*acing the basketball hoop in our driveway, Rick backed up way beyond our foul line.

"Whoa!" I said. "Too far. You can't make that."

But he intently fingered the ball, then rushed a few steps forward and flung it up into the air. It made a perfect arc and swished.

"Hey! Way to go!" I shouted.

It had finally happened. Rick had gotten better than I was at shooting hoops, and it made me grin. Unlike Bill Cosby, who has milked a lot of humor from his anguish at his son's beating him at basketball, I was glad he could better my mediocre shooting.

Rick was making progress in many areas, and Mr. Scheidt, his fifth-grade teacher and a terrific basketball player, modeled academics, sports, and a commitment to Christian values—including humility. For instance, Rick told me Mr. Scheidt admitted he hated spiders.

I learned this because one day I heard Rick talking on the phone to my dad in Pennsylvania. He was telling Granddad that a spider had been discovered in his classroom, and he had volunteered to dispatch it.

When he'd hung up the phone, I asked, "What was that all about?"

"Mr. Scheidt just hates anything creepy-crawley like spiders. A girl saw one and went, 'Auugh!' Mr. Scheidt stepped on it but didn't do much to it. 'I'll get that for you,' I said. So I got a paper towel and picked it up"—here Rick's fingers rose in a grasping motion—"then squished it and threw it away."

"Great, Rick," I said.

"Yes, but I can't stand worms. On the playground I can't stand to step on one."

"Why?"

"Somebody dropped one in my hair once. If someone brings me a worm, I just get out of here!"

Rick seems easy with himself, just matter-of-fact. In school he's in his element. In fact, Mr. Scheidt had said to his class, "There's someone here who is always smiling, cooperative, always helping us, always with a very good attitude! That someone is Rick."

We loved hearing that report, and it put into perspective moments at home when he was bullheaded and argumentative or when he loudly scrapped with his siblings. But the story from school that most intrigued me was when he befriended another boy.

None of Rick's friends would sit with this boy, and Rick demanded to know why they wouldn't. They had no good answer, just said that he was different, in crude, fifth-grade-boy language.

What happened next is what amazed me. Rick walked away from his friends, saying, "Well, if you won't sit with him, then I will." And all by himself he went over and sat with the boy.

Talk about defying peer pressure! *That* takes courage, I thought, and I was proud of Rick. He was maturing and seemed to have found peace, at least at this stage, with his racial identity.

It wasn't that way when he was in first grade. One evening we were standing in front of a mirror and he said to me, "Sometimes I just don't believe the mirror."

"What do you mean?" I asked.

"Sometimes I don't believe I'm really black."

The night before, he'd said as I tucked him in, "I hate my black skin." As he looked into the mirror, it must have seemed surreal to him to be standing next to his white father. And it seemed surreal to me too.

At that moment I felt especially close to him, felt at least a little of what it must be like to live inside his skin, to have white parents and go to a predominantly white school.

Yet his working through all that the next several years may have contributed to the inner strength and perspective to walk away from his buddies and sit down with that boy who was shunned.

But if Rick had forged an identity, Jeanette and I were under no illusions about the crises that might be ahead for all three of our African-American children.

⁓

Sprawled on the family room couch, Rick sat up as Jeanette's and my conversation piqued his interest. "What do you do up there in Communion?" he asked. He was taking the church membership class and knew he would soon be sitting with us in our Scottish form of Communion, in which an elder serves us the bread and cup at a table.

"As we wait, we pray for others taking Communion," Jeanette said.

"And we repent of our sins," I added, "and thank God for his love and forgiveness."

Jeanette asked him what questions he was dealing with in the class.

"What it means to be a Christian," he replied and went into a colorful explanation of just how God blots out sins when we receive Jesus.

"Have you done that?" Jeanette asked.

"Yes."

"When?"

"A couple of years ago." He smiled—a little shyly—his marvelous smile. "And just a little while ago when I was mowing the lawn. Just to make sure."

We grinned. "It was the same with us when we were children," I said. "We had asked Jesus into our lives more than once, 'just to make sure.'"

Rick's inviting Christ to take over his life while mowing the lawn struck me as a marvelous, mundane epiphany. That evening he had been happy at his work, trimming and gathering willow branches, working meaningfully, knowing he was son, brother, and beloved of God. Just weeks shy of eleven, he had a place, a productive place, and was giving himself to Jesus.

What he most urgently wanted to know about his baptism, though, was whether or not Greg would be there. His big brother from college would not only quote Scripture to him but dramatize the stories. He enthusiastically read Narnia books to him and explained how God wanted to be at work in his life.

"Will Greg be there?" he again asked, wanting to nail it down. Greg was just an hour away this summer, working as a counselor at a Christian camp.

"He says he very much wants to," Jeanette answered.

Greg did come on Saturday to help us celebrate Rick's eleventh birthday, and now he was with us on Sunday—Father's Day—for Rick's baptism. Midway through the service our pastor said, "Will the boys and girls who have professed their faith in Christ please come forward with their parents?"

Rick, Jeanette, and I started toward the front, while Greg and Jeanette's mother stayed with Josh and Lindsey. Walking up with Rick to stand beside Bob Harvey, our beloved pastor, seemed wonderfully fitting. He wore over his black clergy robe a symbolic, handwoven, red-and-yellow stole which Greg's high school group had brought back to him from their Guatemala mission trip. Bob had celebrated our adoption of Rick in front of the congregation; I thought of the time Rick was three, sitting beside me and asking if he too could be baptized.

When it came Rick's turn, Bob looked him in the eyes, spoke of Rick's expressed faith, then said, "I baptize you in the name of the Father, the Son, and the Holy Spirit."

Water glistened in beads on Rick's black hair. I thought that Jesus' hair was probably black and glistening as he was baptized by John the Baptist, and I remembered Nouwen's article. The voice Jesus heard as he came out of the Jordan said, "You are my beloved." And now as the last child was baptized, we parents and Bob were joining hands to encircle these children, to put them in the center of the beloved circle. We prayed for them, knowing that they not only were loved by us but were the beloved of the heavenly Father and that Jesus and the Holy Spirit prayed with us for them "with groans that words cannot express" (Rom. 8:26).

As we rejoined the congregation, the big projection screen started lowering. We worshiped in the arts center of a local college, and the screen allowed for huge projections of color slides.

We now saw a series of photos of Rick's confirmation class, lively candid shots of the baptized children as they learned, played, and laughed together: young men, young women, linked with each other, their faith, and their church family. *What a great group of friends for Rick to have,* I thought, *and what marvelous opportunities before him!*

Suddenly a gigantic shot of Rick with his magnetic smile filled the front of the auditorium. For a long time they kept his image on the screen, this huge photo of a maturing young man embracing his church family with love and faith.

This was just like Rick's and Kwame's faces in my dream. Bigger than life, vivid, powerful. But on this Father's Day, instead of it hitting me with wrenching sadness, here was faith and hope. Fifteen feet tall in the projected photo, our son Rick, this young black male, descendant of Mississippi slaves, looked down on all of us as if pronouncing a healing benediction.

chapter nineteen

*C*lunk! I slowly eased my station wagon onto the dirt road toward my father's home, but the gully at its beginning was deeper than ever. I pressed the gas pedal, and the undercarriage scraped as our headlights stabbed above the same rocks I had so often dodged as a college student in my '49 Plymouth.

Todd had helped drive the fourteen hours from Chicago. Now married, he wanted to help me move Dad to Wheaton. Slowly we drove past the sound of frogs in Prosser's Lake.

"Think he'll be awake?" Todd asked.

"Doesn't matter. He always takes a nap anyway before going to bed."

I drove up the steep driveway, parked in my usual spot, and clicked on the interior lights. Had he heard us? We tidied the car and collected our gear.

No lights came on. "Should we tap the horn a little?" Todd asked.

"Let's just go in."

We got out, knocked, then opened the door. It was strange arriving home without a joyous welcome. When Mom was alive, the lights would flash on before the car stopped. She'd rush to the door with Dad close behind, there'd be hugs all around, and into the kitchen we'd go for soup or bread and cheese. Even last year when I came with the little children, Dad had been ready for us. But this time cancer had weakened him.

"Hi, Dad," I called into the dimly lighted room.

"Oh," he said, waking up. "Didn't hear you." He pulled himself up from his chair and we hugged.

He felt small in my arms, his bones distinct against my chest. "Want anything to eat?" he asked.

"No," Todd said, "we've been eating—"

"Well," Dad interrupted, "you may not like the food here. I fired the cook!"

Dad chuckled—he was the cook—and we laughed with him. He preferred anyone's cooking to his own. Dad was shy but he was full of humor and determination. At ninety-one he still drove his ancient Buick up and down these mountains and still visited Richie in prison.

Knowing red squirrels had invaded his attic, I asked him about them.

"They're taking over!" he lamented. "They've eaten holes in the ceiling tiles."

"Well, don't worry," Todd said. "After tomorrow it won't matter."

Dad nodded. After he left, the house and land would revert to the U.S. government as part of the Delaware Water Gap National Recreation Area. "That's right," he said cheerfully. "Now it's the government's problem."

Next morning I awoke in "my room." Dad had completed it when I started college at the nearby university. My feet hit the beautiful hardwood floor Dad had laid, and my eyes roved over the furniture I'd assembled and finished more than forty years before. On the walls Mom had hung, to an embarrassing degree, photos and plaques from my career. But stacked on the desk I'd made were also plaques Richie had won in prison sports activities. Richie had no one else—only Mom would give his achievements recognition.

But now the room would be bulldozed with the rest of the house, this lovely home in which so many had found nurture and love.

At breakfast I said, "You know, Dad, it's exactly fifty years ago this month we moved up here from Camden."

"That so?"

When we had moved from Camden, the house had been little more than a hunter's cabin. Our only water was from a shallow well with a hand pump way down by the road. "Remember what we used to prime the pump when we forgot to save water for priming?"

"Pea juice," Dad answered immediately.

"Yup. We'd open a can, pour the juice in, and pump like mad!"

Dad smiled. "I remember you and Johnny didn't want indoor plumbing. You were happy just using the outhouse. Even in the dead of winter."

I wrapped my hands around my hot coffee mug. "We got used to it, even with all those daddy longlegs. Actually, I kind of liked them." I looked around at the cozy breakfast nook and the big hospitality room beyond it. "Dad, it's incredible what you did here, building this house room by room all by yourself on evenings and weekends."

He nodded, then cleared the dishes. His suitcases had been carefully packed for days. Todd joined us and we started filling boxes.

By late morning we were nearly done. I took a break and walked the familiar dirt road one last time.

I stopped by my grandfather's deserted, collapsing house. More than forty years ago I had found him sprawled in his kitchen, dead. Beside his house was his trailer, where Richie had hidden the days before he had panicked and shot Mrs. Prosser.

I walked on to Prosser's Lake, actually a one-acre pond, still much as it was when my brother and I had watched Mr. Prosser having it made in the fifties. I stood on a little cement dock where, as little boys, Todd and Greg and later Rick and Josh fished out little sunnys. Here is where Joshua at age two, while blowing bubbles from a wand, tottered into the water and cut his tongue so badly that it bled all over his shirt and made him sick the rest of the day.

Across the road is a tall evergreen, one half scorched away. Vandals had burned the Prosser home when it stood deserted. The old barn too was gone, and I thought of the way Mr. Prosser, a stockbroker and amateur artist, had painted on it a gigantic scene of two boys schussing down the mountain. Johnny and I knew as we passed it every day on the school bus that he had been thinking of us as he painted.

Close down the road was the site of Mrs. Prosser's home. Here she had told Richie she would call the police. Here he had panicked and used the shotgun, then fled. Here Mrs. Prosser had bled to death on this gravel driveway.

Now only the gravel remained in the weed-grown homesite. Flashes of yellow—goldfinches—rushed through it past black-eyed Susans and wild cherry blossoms.

~

Back in Illinois Dad was our gentle, unassuming guest, grateful for everything we did for him. But he was losing weight every week.

He sat quietly in a big power recliner from hospice. "I love you, Dad," I said.

"I love you, too, Son."

We said this to each other more now. Hugs. Words. Yet all inadequate to express this enormous event of slowly dying. I felt as if we were at some airport gate waiting, waiting, waiting. Suddenly the call would come for the lone passenger to walk down the ramp all by himself. Dad would go. I would stay. Dad would step over a line. We'd be in different worlds.

For a while, at least.

What's it really like on the other side? What happens to us when we arrive?

"Dad, what do you think the next life will be like?"

His well-worn Bible is beside him. He knows all the standard answers. He's a reader and a thinker, and he knows there's a lot of mystery in the universe and in things of faith. "Hard to know," he said.

"Do you feel you'll be welcomed? Do you feel apprehensive?"

His answer jarred me. Quietly he said, "Well, we're all bad boys, you know."

I did know that. So did he dread meeting God? He had never been as intently religious as Mom or, for that matter, me. But he had surely embraced Christ and always lived faithfully, never judging, always helping anybody and everybody.

I thought of Augustine saying we have nothing to give to God but our wretchedness and his mercy. And Ambrose, when dying and being asked if he was afraid of God's judgment, saying, "We have a good master."

"I hear you, Dad," I said. "Yes, we're all bad boys. And the closer we get to God, the more we realize it. But that's the whole point of grace."

We talked then about grace, that we deserve none of it. And we talked about that old song about a yellow ribbon. Years ago when I'd hear it, I'd get tears in my eyes because of its joyous expression of grace. A released prisoner is riding home on a bus, not knowing if he will be accepted or rejected. He's written his girl that if she forgives him, she should "tie a yellow ribbon 'round the old oak tree." If there's no yellow ribbon, he'll just ride by.

On the bus he's full of anxiety. The passengers share his feelings. Suddenly the whole busload of people cheers as the forgiven man sees not one but a *hundred* yellow ribbons on that old oak tree! The one he loves not only forgives him but exuberantly welcomes him home.

For Dad I saw yellow ribbons and joyous welcome. Here comes John Myra! Let angels shout! Joy! Joy!

I prayed he'd feel that way as he waited here at the gate with me, as he was moving straight into the arms of God.

A few days later I was talking with Dad when the phone rang. I stepped behind his chair to pick it up and heard the excited voice of Shari Maxwell. She and her husband, Shawn, had just received word that everything was set for them to fly to Ethiopia.

Shawn and Shari were a young couple who more than once had sat in our living room discussing whether or not they should adopt. Now after a long process the decks were cleared for their getting the infant girl and little boy soon to become their children. Shari's parents, our good friends Jim and Carol Pluedemann of Sudan Interior Mission, had already visited the children at the mission hospital.

Jeanette joined us on the other phone, and we heard details of their great adventure: Shawn and Shari would travel seventeen hours via Washington and Rome to get there. The beautiful Ethiopian girl and boy whose photos graced our bulletin board would be coming soon to their new home in Wheaton.

These two children were being rescued from circumstances in which they would have almost surely died.

It reminded me of a visit a half dozen years before by Keith Coats of YFC in South Africa. He had greeted me in my office and soon noticed the photos of our children. Immediately he asked questions and I shared a little of the adoption stories.

After Keith returned to South Africa, I'd received a letter from him saying he and his wife had adopted an abandoned baby. He wrote that our conversation had helped them make their decision, and enclosed was a photo of the new Coats family: father, mother, two small white children, and a little black boy.

All over the world were such children without homes, I thought, and bless the Maxwells and the Coatses—and the many others like them.

But it was my nature, even as I thought of the joy of Shari and Shawn's adoption, to think also of all the unrescued kids. I'd read one estimate that an astounding hundred million kids lived on the world's streets. The size of the problem was paralyzing.

When I'd think such thoughts, I'd remember Mother Teresa. When someone would say that the suffering of India was such a vast ocean of need that caring for the dying was hopeless, she told them she was in the subtraction business. She would simply show Jesus' love to one person at a time.

And when his love is shown, the ripples of his peace start to go everywhere. One action creates another.

A week later Jeanette, the kids, and I stood at a restaurant entrance. Our good friends Vic and Betsey Glavach had come with us to celebrate my birthday, and Vic had borrowed a medi-van with a lift. He had my wheelchair-bound dad in the lift and was lowering it.

Thud! The lift hit the sidewalk and Dad said cheerfully, "Now that's service!"

Rick and Josh thought this action was great and were anxious to press that lift button, too, so Vic gave them each a turn.

As we entered the restaurant, it was obvious that Dad had slipped dramatically. He couldn't make it across a room without help. We wheeled him to the back of the restaurant, where our group filled a long table.

Out the windows we could see the CTI office buildings I'd worked in for more than twenty years. The complex had grown a great deal since our move from Washington, D.C. Then we published just one magazine, now a dozen. The pace was quickening: we'd acquired two more magazines the past spring. More than 150 people were crammed into those buildings. Pressure, pressure, pressure. The growth was both energizing and exhausting.

We were now purchasing land for a new publishing complex. With growth accelerating, I needed to stay vitally engaged. Sometimes it felt as if juggling the pressures of fatherhood and career couldn't be done.

A comic strip invaded my mind. The strip always starts with a weary father yanked on by squalling kids. Pain evident on his face, he asks the reader, "Why me?"

Yes, why me? Most other men my age go home to a quiet house. I'm the one who desperately craves solitude. I hate going to ball games and school functions—always have. Other parents love this stuff.

Yet why not me? Lots of adoptive parents make far greater sacrifices, adopting despite crushing challenges. And as I looked at those buildings, I understood that few men my age had it easy. Every husband and father I knew carried large burdens—including Vic sitting beside me.

I thought also of a black couple in our community, the Odoms. After raising six sons, in retirement they adopted four more small children. As I sat there celebrating birthday number fifty-nine, Nathaniel Odom, eighty-three, and his wife, Zady, seventy-two, were raising kids ages twelve, nine, seven, and six. Nathaniel and I matched—except I didn't have a nine-year-old, and I wasn't eighty-three!

Oswald Chambers talks in his books about God's ignoring our "natural affinities" as he "engineers circumstances." When we try to dodge the drudgery, we miss God's "glorious opportunity."

Chambers is bracing. Whenever I feel self-pity rising, I can count on him to quash it. He declares that we're to be broken bread and poured-out wine for others and we can't choose how, that grapes only become wine when they've been crushed, yet God packs our lives with wondrous surprises.

Lindsey too was always surprising me, and one night the irony of her plan for my life put all this into humorous perspective. I was tucking her in and hugged her tight, saying, "I love you very, very much, and I always will."

She wanted to keep me talking, so she said, "But I love you even more. I love you hundreds and hundreds and bunches of hundreds! Isn't that a lot?"

"Yes, that's a lot."

I was leaving the room but she wanted me to stay. Abruptly she said, "Daddy, you might have lots of grandchildren. Maybe I'll have quintuplets!" She enthusiastically hiked herself up on the bed. "I'll go to work and you can take care of them."

What? Now here was the future I'd always dreamed of: caring for quintuplets every day, perhaps in my seventies, while my daughter went to work.

Apparently Lindsey thought this would be very appealing, and she started describing how it would work. "You'll have two on your lap that you're feeding. And you'll have two watching TV and one playing."

The mental image danced before me and I smiled. "Lindsey, let me get this straight. You'll go to work and I'll stay home with your five kids?"

What she said next nearly doubled me up with laughter.

"Yes," she said firmly. "You'll love it! Two on your lap!"

chapter twenty

*O*ne of the guests at Michelle's wedding had been Jeanette's sister's husband, Dirk. Not long afterward this young father had died of cancer.

At his funeral in Anderson, Indiana, his daughter Shallen had sung a beautiful tribute to him, and his son had chosen a song of father-son love that brought tears throughout the congregation. After the service I had watched as hundreds came up to hug Jeanette's bereaved sister Marita and her two children. The sense of community had been unmistakable.

A few years later Marita fell in love with Scott, a widower. At the rehearsal dinner for their wedding, Scott had led all the celebrants in line dancing—a rollicking good time for everyone. The wedding was a beautiful blend of two families coming together in faith.

However, before the first year of their marriage was over, Scott was diagnosed with cancer. His leg was amputated. Scott was remarkably plucky, emerging from the process cancer free and continuing his work with a prosthesis.

Now we were back in Anderson to celebrate Shallen's wedding to Chris. Two pastors were officiating, for the groom's father had also passed away. Each pastor had known one of the fathers and spoke eloquently of the rich Christian heritage they had passed on.

Sitting with our family and aunts and cousins near the front, it was hard not to think of the funeral for Shallen's dad, held in this same church. I thought, *Dirk isn't here to give away his daughter, but Dirk and Shallen's closeness remains. There are a lot of Dirk's best qualities in that girl, and she's carrying all those lessons with her today.*

The pastors' tributes to the fathers blended in with wise words for the bride and groom. I wondered how much Rick, Josh, and Lindsey were absorbing. Two fathers who had spiritually blazed the way for this young couple. A stepfather with grit and faith. Two pastors with hope and challenge. A community of faith that transcended grief and tragedy.

Back in our kitchen in Illinois I poured orange juice into Lindsey's pink elephant mug. "You know," she said as she picked it up, "some people don't know there's a God."

"That's true," I said, thinking the wedding had made an impression on her.

"They're lucky."

"Oh?" I was puzzled at that. "What do you mean?"

"They don't have to worry about it," she said. "They don't have to worry about going to hell."

I put down the juice carton. "Do you worry about going to hell?"

"Sure."

I looked at this girl who was always wondering about God and how to do right and had prayed the sinner's prayer and whose mind cascaded with questions. I said, "You don't have to worry, you know." And thus started more dialogue with my little searching theologian.

"Time to brush your teeth," I finally announced. "Michelle will read to you and tuck you in." Michelle and Greg were both in town for the wedding.

"Daddy," she interrupted, "you have more gray hairs!" She began inspecting my head with her fingers.

"Actually, you can't find many," I said.

She hugged me tight. "Daddy, I can't stop hugging you. Every time I look at you, I think you are going to die before Mommy, so that's why I have to hug you more." She knew Shallen's and Chris's fathers had died much younger than me, and she saw how much I resembled my dad.

Yet as she hugged me, I thought, *God knew my age when he barged into my life with his adoption plans. Shouldn't I trust him? Am I too old and too white?* Recently we had been jolted by the news that another girl

Lindsey's age had lost her young, black father, Spencer Perkins. Like his father, John Perkins, who had been so brutally beaten by police in the sixties, Spencer had worked tirelessly for racial reconciliation, but he had collapsed and died of heart failure.

No, worrying was foolish—and the truth was, Lindsey was not morose at all. In fact, she seemed rather cheerful. Suddenly she declared, "Daddy, I wish you could live for ten thousand years!"

I scooped her up in my arms and gave her a long hug. "So do I, Lindsey—ten thousand years with you. And we *will* both live ten thousand years, and a lot more."

She knew I meant heaven, but our talking was interrupted by a mighty crash above us.

I carried Lindsey to the bottom of the stairs. "Okay, you guys," I called. "That's enough!" College man Greg, a gymnastics instructor, had obviously been doing stuff with Rick and Josh that belonged in the gym.

"Josh, time to brush your teeth," I said as I climbed the steps.

Greg and Rick went to the basement to continue their horseplay. Rick had said to me once, "I hope Greg doesn't get married until he's twenty-nine. Then he'll still play with me." I pointed out to him that Todd, though married, still played matchbox cars with him—but he wanted as much attention from the big boys as he could get.

"Come on, Josh, it's just you and me," I said as he tried to follow Greg and Rick to the basement for more rough-and-tumble. I read to him the hilarious *Little Rabbit FooFoo,* then a cutout booklet he made in kindergarten about a snowman. Once again we read about Jonah and the whale—for some reason Josh always wanted the tale of Jonah from the Bible storybook my dad had given him years ago.

Reading done, he cartwheeled down the hall, then dropped to his haunches and leaped like a frog. I picked him up and felt his muscles, tight like rubber bands from gymnastics. His nightshirt was a yellow Nike T with a big rainbow I'd bought twenty years ago, then passed on to Todd, then he to Josh. "You sure are all muscles," I said.

In response he grabbed me around the neck with an iron grip. Every night he wanted to test his endurance—and mine. I arched my body over his bed and let him hang from my neck. "You're getting heavier," I complained. "You're getting too strong!"

Finally his grip broke and he fell into his pillow. "Tell me a Thomas story," he asked.

I'm not very good at Thomas the Tank Engine stories—I'd rather make up crazy fantasy tales. But I told Josh one anyway. After that he said, "Dad, are we getting another baby?"

Josh absolutely loves babies and is always lobbying for another one. "Would you like that?"

"Yes!" He gave me a huge smile.

"Would you like a boy or a girl?"

He hesitated for just a moment, then said, "A boy."

As I tucked him in and let him know for the fiftieth time we weren't getting a baby anytime soon, I thought of Josh someday perhaps raising many black children himself.

Passing Lindsey's door, I heard Michelle's voice reading. Over the past six years Michelle has given Lindsey wonderful books, starting with one for "your very first Christmas as my sister." She often sent Josh and Lindsey *Gullah Gullah* videotapes and always told them on the phone, "I love you bunches!" She was a great cheerleader for Jeanette—when things got tough, she'd say, "You're doing great, Mom!" *It's a benediction having her here,* I thought, listening to my beautiful blond daughter reading and laughing with my beautiful brown daughter.

I went downstairs and heard Greg and Rick still wrestling in the basement. Greg had urged us to send Rick out to spend a week with him in Boston. He was always challenging Rick spiritually.

Todd too had bonded with his little siblings. The previous week Jeanette and I had not been able to join the family for our annual Wisconsin vacation because of Dad's need for twenty-four-hour care. Todd, with wife Lisa and with Greg, had taken charge of the little kids that week. And the year before, when Jeanette had phoned Todd about designating in our will a church family as guardians of our kids, Todd had immediately said, "No way!"

"Then who should have them if something happens to us?" Jeanette asked.

"We should!"

Jeanette knew the kids would greatly prefer that. "But what would Lisa say?"

From the background Jeanette heard Lisa's response. "Well, of course!"

So we naturally changed our will.

With Josh and Lindsey tucked in, I sat down beside Dad, who was asleep in his recliner. *Despite grief and pain,* I thought, *we are blessed.* Yet I was acutely aware that we were not an idyllic family. "Life is difficult," said Scott Peck. Another book could be written about all our children's pains and the struggles that blindsided us. Our birth children went through deep waters, and we anticipate the same—maybe more so— for our adopted children.

Yet a quote from de Caussade rolls through my mind. "Those who have abandoned themselves to God lead mysterious lives and receive from him exceptional and miraculous gifts—by means of the most ordinary, natural and chance experiences."

Dad always insisted on coming to church, but he was growing extremely weak. On Communion Sunday we placed his wheelchair beside us. "Dad," I said quietly, "we'll go up to the Communion table. Someone will come to serve you here."

Up front Rick sat beside me at the table. By "chance" it was elder Paul Erickson, the dad of Rick's best friend, who offered us the bread and the cup. I thought, *Whatever happens ahead, whatever Rick's troubles or successes, here he has sat with fathers in communion with our Father through Jesus Christ his Son.*

As we descended to our seats, I saw an elder administering the sacraments to my father. Surely, I thought, this was Dad's last Communion.

Dad was hallucinating. The cancer in his brain made him see— really see—persons and creatures standing beside him or hovering near the ceiling. At bedtime he insisted that it was morning and that we were cruel to insist he sleep. "You're all screwballs," he would say.

"You're a screwball. I'm a screwball." Despite his malfunctioning brain, he seemed able to separate himself from it and realize he wasn't right.

I walked over to Dad's hospital bed by our fireplace. "How're you doing?" I asked.

"Okay." His hand was reaching up toward the ceiling as if he were working a piece of machinery. Up and down, up and down, he intently worked on his imaginary project.

Out of the blue Dad asked, "How's your father?"

Did I hear him right? What was he thinking?

"Who am I?" I asked him.

"You're my father," he said.

I felt very strange as I sat down on his bed beside him. Eighty years ago in Norway his young father had died. Now Dad was a boy again, back with his father.

Years before, Dad had given me the ceramic milk cup he had used as a baby. On it two little boys wave Norwegian flags over the words *Flink Gut*—smart boy. As a child, I'd looked at it often. It seemed to have come from the beginning of time. Now I was twice as old as Dad was when he became my father.

How strange that now the early 1900s seemed not nearly so long ago. In fact, they seemed just a little further back than Camden in the forties.

A year before as Dad and I hiked a mountain—he wasn't even puffing at ninety—he had told me about his young father's kidney failure. "He knew he was dying," Dad said, the old memory from Norway still fresh. A few years after his father's death, he and his mother had come to America.

Dad seemed content in the bed, his arm outstretched and his fingers busy, his mind elsewhere. Recently in the middle of the night Dad had stretched his arms wide and called out, "Momma! Momma! Come!"

His mother had died when she was half the age of the old man now calling for her. Dad's deep cry in the night for his mother filled me with a longing to reunite them, to have him feel her embrace and know her love again.

All those years ago he was her only child. Now he was not ninety-one but a boy again—about to burst from these old bones and merge into a new body for a fabulous reunion.

⁓

Days later I finished a phone conversation with my brother, then walked over to Dad's slumped figure in the bed. "Dad, looks as if Johnny and Donna won't get here until Wednesday."

I didn't expect a response. He had been mostly sleeping and hallucinating. But he said to me very quietly, "I don't know if I have that long."

It was the first time he had acknowledged he was very close to death. Though he'd spoken, his eyes were closed. Wednesday was five days away.

Each of the next five days we thought might be his last. He mostly slept and couldn't communicate except for the odd vagaries of his mind.

Wednesday we heard Johnny and Donna at the front door. We greeted them, then explained that Dad was sleeping and that when he was awake, he was in another world.

However, as soon as they entered the family room, we all heard Dad say in a clear voice, "Hello, Johnny. Hello, Donna."

They hugged him and he responded lucidly, as if he had just returned from somewhere else. The words and smiles flowed back and forth, and for the rest of the day, when he was not sleeping, Dad talked with us and even kidded us a little.

Next day Johnny and I stood beside his bed, and Jeanette aimed her camera. "Let's get Dad and his boys smiling," she commanded. And Dad, despite his extreme weakness and gaunt face, forced out a big smile for Jeanette to capture.

Friday, midmorning, Dad seemed worn out and was deeply asleep. Johnny and Donna came to his bed and said their final good-byes.

A few hours later, just after lunch, Rick, Josh, Lindsey, and I were watching a *National Geographic* special. I looked over at Dad and thought he looked very still. I studied the covers over his chest. They didn't seem to be moving.

I got up and walked closer to him. Finally I took his hand and felt no pulse.

I thought, *Dad just drifted away from us as we sat here. He's actually gone.*

I lowered his hand and got Jeanette. After checking him, she said quietly, "Kids, Granddad's gone."

The boys asked some questions. Lindsey wanted to know if she could touch him.

"Of course you can," Jeanette said.

Lindsey slowly walked over to Dad's motionless form and stroked his arm and hand. She stood beside him, awed and tearful with her thoughts.

Jeanette made the call to hospice.

So, I thought, it was just as people said. Dad really had hung on just long enough to say good-bye to Johnny and Donna. I stared at my father's face and blessed him from the depths of my soul. Quiet, loving, always a peacemaker, now he was experiencing a far greater peace.

Jeanette dug papers from her desk. I listened for the inevitable ring of the doorbell. Neither of us was aware that Lindsey had gone into the kitchen and in her grieving was making her own transition. The tears were dried on her face, and somehow she was sensing the exuberance of Dad's entry into heaven, for she began singing softly:

He's happy now!
Granddad's up in heaven!
He's happy now!

I stepped into the kitchen. "That's right, Lindsey. You are so, so right." She began singing again, her feet moving and her eyes sparkling.

Granddad's up in heaven.
He's happy now!
Granddad's jumpin' the mountain.
He's happy now!

Her little body was moving with rhythm and sound in a lively tune that perfectly matched the words. The music and words entered our grief like white doves in darkness.

The hospice people and the funeral director arrived, and the chaplain spent time with each child. Then after everyone had left, I asked

Lindsey if she could sing her song again. She hesitated, but then she began again, spontaneous phrases tumbling out of her mouth as she sang her six-year-old faith:

Granddad's up in heaven.
   He's happy now!
So-oh-oh
   Granddad's jumping into God's arms,
Happy in heaven.
   He's happy now!
Jumping into the angel's arms,
   He's happy now!
He's marrying his wife again.
   He's happy now!

As Lindsey sang those last two lines, my smile became as big as hers. "That's wonderful! That's right!" I said to her. "He's with my momma again." (I wasn't going to question the marrying part.) Lindsey kept singing new verses, pouring out all her feelings, hips and arms swinging, words matching her rhythm.

Granddad's in heaven.
   He's happy now!
I'm so glad he didn't go to Lu-ci-fer—
   He's happy now!
Granddad's up there with Ga-bri-el.
   He's happy now!
I love him lots and lots.
   He's the best granddad in the world.
He's the only granddad in my world.
   Just when he died today,
My mom and my dad cried.
   It was so sad seeing him. . . .

Lindsey sang for me and all my struggles in this world of joy mixed with dying, this world of surreal good-byes yet great hopes. Her feelings spilled out in words and music that resonated in their simplicity.

I'm so glad he went to heaven.
　　I want him here more days.
I wish he didn't have the pain.
　　I wish he stayed more days.
I wish he never
　　Started to die.
But Granddad's in heaven.
　　He's happy now!
Granddad's in heaven.
　　He's happy now!

finale

The day after New Year's, the worst blizzard in thirty years struck Chicago. We watched the snow blowing and heaping up outside, but in the family room where Dad had died, we were warm and content. Rick flopped on the couch beside me. With a nod and a wink, Jeanette motioned for me to tickle him to liven him up.

Rick smiled when I made a halfhearted jab at his ribs. Jeanette threw a wad of paper at him. "You are so cute when you smile, Rick!"

He erased the smile but it was still dancing in his eyes. He asked if he could call Todd in Minneapolis, then went upstairs to make the call.

"Glad he talks to his big brothers," I said. "Worth every nickel. Maybe we'll have to put in direct lines when he hits adolescence!"

Jeanette shrugged and nodded. We knew that very tough times might be ahead, but for now soccer and social life at school seemed to be keeping him energized and comfortable with his identity.

I went upstairs to my den; Josh saw me and followed me in. *The Snowy Day* was one of the books on the pile, and considering all the snow blowing around outside, it seemed a perfect time to read it to him. As I opened the book, I pointed to the many shapes on the first page and asked him, "Did you know that no two snowflakes are alike? That every snowflake is different?"

"Every one?" he asked.

"Yes. Every single one is different."

Silence.

I turned some more pages, including ones showing mountains of snow. "Really?" he asked. "Every one?"

"Yes, really. If you put each flake under a microscope, you'd see each is different from all the others."

More silence.

Finally Josh looked up at me with raised eyebrows that said he might just have figured out my game. He then said in a lyrical, quizzical, bombastic way, "You're making all this up!"

The way he said it just broke me up. I was laughing too hard to talk, so I grabbed him and rubbed his hair. He laughed with me and obviously loved it that he had made me laugh so hard.

Children can bring a lot of stress. But sometimes they can just blow it all away.

Later Lindsey and I were coloring and doing math workbooks in the family room. I got up and went into the kitchen. Then as I returned and eased myself onto the couch beside her, she said with a little smile and a cock of her head, "I love it when I hear slippers coming."

Did I hear her right? What was she saying?

"Why?" I asked. "Why do you love it when you hear slippers?"

She grinned and looked into my eyes. "Because I know that means you are coming."

I blinked and looked down at the big floppy slippers on my feet. Once again I was amazed at this child, my heart captured by this precious little daughter who had entered my life so unexpectedly.

The adventure of faith draws us into mystery and includes great and mighty things. But often the greatest things in our lives are rather small.

We just have to have eyes to see. . . .

afterword

As Jeanette and I were finishing our bread pudding in the Sister Bay Cafe in Door County, Wisconsin, I felt a longing for my parents to join us at the table. "Mom would have absolutely loved this place," I said, looking at wall hangings of fjords, stavekirks, Norwegian flags, and Velkommen embroidery. "Everything Norwegian."

We stepped from the cafe into its gift shop with reindeer sweaters, Rosemaling paintings, recipe books. As Jeanette looked at sweaters, I turned, then stopped and stared at a piece of framed art. Recognition rippled through me, and then a smile that became a laugh.

"Jeanette, you've got to see this."

In colorful calligraphy with prancing elk on the border were these words:

> *A Norwegian*
> *has an abiding sense of*
> *TRAGEDY*
> *which sustains him*
> *through temporary periods of*
> *JOY*

Jeanette studied it, smiled, then pronounced firmly, "That's you, all right! It's perfect!"

She walked off to inspect some red mugs in a bin, but I kept staring at the words. When she returned, I said, "Sounds just like Garrison Keillor, and he couldn't have said it better. He's always talking about Norwegians at Lake Wobegon."

"You've got to buy it!"

I walked around the shop but kept returning to the calligraphy. Jeanette came up behind me. "Go ahead. Get it."

We brought it to the register. As the man wrapped it, he explained how he had started work here. The owner had told him, "I need an old Norwegian for the shop." He had replied, "Well, I'm an old Norwegian!"

He reminded me of my grandfather. As he wrapped five bargain red mugs for us, I considered how close to his age I was getting—and caught myself. More melancholic thoughts! The calligraphy was right.

Back at our time-share condo, as Jeanette arranged photos in an album, I couldn't shut off my brain. The restaurant reminded me of Johan and Hjordis and other relatives in Norway: hospitable, sensible, full of life and humor and love for the outdoors. What a rich heritage I had. Words like *Viking* conjured up heroics and grand adventure. And scholars say Leif Erickson really did beat Columbus to the New World. How bracing to be of Viking stock!

Yet also sobering. I thought about European Christians in Viking times. To them, the appearance of longboats was their most horrible nightmare. They prayed daily to escape the Vikings' rape and pillage. This included—who can believe this?—"the popular sport of tossing infants from spear point to spear point."

Could ancestors of mine really have done that? What a mixed heritage to be of Viking stock!

I looked at Jeanette working on the photos and thought of Nordic-looking Becky in high school, who had been so ashamed of her frizzy hair and mixed genes. Now my family was mixed like hers. Could we honor black pride and Norse pride and Jeanette's English heritage? Could we be part of getting past all the tribalism and religious hatreds shattering so many lives around the world?

Maybe our country would never get past them. Despite so many efforts at racial reconciliation, black rage and white backlash just seemed to be getting worse. Some African-Americans still demanded reparations, which most whites thought fruitless. Some blacks said slavery may have been terrible, but it was better than being left in Africa— an opinion that infuriated other blacks. The vision of Archbishop

Mundia's white and black piano keys making beautiful music seemed rare indeed.

The country's and the world's troubles were so intractable, and Jeanette and I could do so comparatively little. Sure, we had adopted three children, but what about the world's hundred million kids living and dying on the streets?

I often thought of a T. S. Eliot story. The great poet was at a party, and a woman next to him at the table said, "Isn't the party wonderful?"

"Yes," Eliot had replied, "if you see the essential horror of it all."

The poet's startling response often resonated in me. We who are at the party experience little of the world's horrors.

These thoughts churned in my mind as Jeanette wrote captions on photos. "Here, you've got to look at this!" she exclaimed, holding up a shot of Greg, Rick, Josh, and Lindsey. "Are they cute or what?"

I stepped over to the table strewn with albums and pictures. Cheerful scenes and beloved faces drew me in. Here was joy.

"The little kids sure love Greg!" Jeanette said.

I nodded. "And Michelle and Todd," I said. "But maybe this week that's running thin!" We smiled because Michelle and Todd were each taking a half week to baby-sit for us and might need to discipline them.

"The adoptions have been good for our birth kids," Jeanette said with a decisive lift of her chin. "They're gonna make great parents!"

"Definitely. But Michelle told me reading the book manuscript was painful, especially the parts about Kwame. And Greg said, 'It hurts so much.'"

Jeanette paused in her photo shuffling. "It sure does. Our big kids felt plenty of loss. But they grew through it. And think about Todd's sermon."

Todd was finishing his fourth year of seminary and had preached a sermon titled "Praise God We're Adopted." He had told Karba's story and, quoting Ephesians, said the good news was that God had chosen us to be adopted into his family.

We looked at more photos—Jeanette had piles of them spread across the table. Some of them captured our children's story better than did words. "Terrific shots," I said. "You've been the driving force in the adoptions. Maybe you should have written this book. You're a good writer, you know."

Instantly she said, "No way! I couldn't possibly sit that long!"

Jeanette was a person of action. When a neighbor was dying of cancer, when another had to be rushed to the emergency room, she was there. When a couple in our church birthed a deformed baby, she was first to their hospital room.

"We really are wired differently," I said.

Jeanette didn't worry about all the world's children, but she'd jump right in and care for the ones at her doorstep. Yet her energy had limits. When the kids fought or disobeyed, she'd get frustrated and tired. Since we had raised our birth children, demands on parents had escalated and the culture encouraged nasty attitudes and bad talk. Too often we both felt overwhelmed. We were not naive; each of our three little kids was demonstrating that we had large challenges ahead.

"Someone asked me how we do it," I said. "How we handle it all. I told him, 'Well, we're barely doing it.'"

Jeanette went over to the couch and flopped down. "What frustrates me is, people think, 'Oh, Jeanette, you just love babies, you asked for all this, quit your bellyaching.' But I wasn't stupid—I knew babies grow into teenagers."

"I don't hear you bellyaching. Who hears you bellyaching?"

Jeanette shrugged. "Not many, I hope. But people think it was all my idea, that I talked you into it. Actually, it was God's idea. All I was going to do was short-term care for sick babies. But now I'm expected to keep up with the mothers twenty years younger, doing all the school and sports activities and homework and parties. And we have no grandparents to help us—Mom's eighty."

She stretched herself out full length on the sofa; I sat down next to the fireplace. "So how do you cope?"

"I'll tell you how. By getting out of the house and helping someone else. When you sit with a woman who's dying, it brings perspective. Compared to some of my friends, my life is a breeze."

I nodded. I thought of some months ago when we'd had a man and his wife over for picnic supper in our backyard. Jeanette was assuring the husband that as his wife's cancer progressed, she'd be there for them. I was wondering how she could promise that—but for months as the mother of three was dying, Jeanette was right there helping the family.

"People must wonder how you find time to break away."

"I've got to break away, to get out of myself!" Suddenly Jeanette bounced up off the couch and with a grin flung her arms straight up and stretched high. "And to make myself feel younger, sometimes I drive Mom and her eighty-year-old friends around. They tell me, 'Oh, how young and energetic you are! You're so cute and wonderful.' Who wouldn't want to hear that?"

I grinned back at her, and Jeanette looked out the window at the lake. "And we cope by coming here to Door County! And we have to look for the fun!"

That was her code phrase for remembering advice Jane Sorenson had given her years before. Jane had been Jeanette's cancer patient in the hospital and had experienced painful procedures and loss. In addition her daughter became schizophrenic, was institutionalized, and was later brutally attacked. Jane's cancer reoccurred. Once when Jeanette asked her how she coped with it all, a twinkle came into Jane's eyes and she said, "You have to look for the fun!"

Now, decades later, Jane still has her bedrock faith and that twinkle in her eye. "Only Jane could go through all that and say, 'Look for the fun,'" Jeanette said.

"She's incredible," I agreed. "Deep. Prayerful. Never loses her spirit."

Jeanette marked another photo. "So where's the fun for us?"

"How about the time Josh couldn't wait for a birthday party and asked me, 'How do you make three days go by really, really fast?'"

"Sometimes the questions he asks me on the way to gymnastics really make me laugh," Jeanette said.

I picked up a close-up of Lindsey in our backyard. "Remember when we were up here with the kids, and Lindsey said she knew what she wanted to do to the Devil? She said, 'At midnight I'd go to the Devil's room and check if he was asleep. Then I'd go to the farm and get a bucket of muddy pigs and put them in his underwear drawer!'"

Jeanette and I laughed again, remembering the moment. "When I heard that, it cracked me up," I said. "Where'd she get that idea? A bucket of pigs in the Devil's underwear drawer!"

"Did Rick tell you about the way he made his class laugh?"

"No."

"Mr. Otterby came up to me at school and asked if I'd heard about Rick." Mr. Otterby was a big teddy bear of a coach and teacher, and I envisioned him approaching Jeanette with his hearty grin. "He told me a teacher had asked in Rick's class what mammal couldn't jump." With a smile Jeanette raised her eyebrows and asked me, "Do you know the answer?"

I thought a moment and couldn't come up with one. "No. What's the answer?"

"Well, the class couldn't think of one, either. But then Rick raised his hand and said, "White men can't jump!""

I burst out laughing and Jeanette joined me, saying, "Rick's class just roared! And Mr. Otterby thought it was really, really funny."

"It's perfect," I said. "Hilarious."

"We just have to hang on to those stories!"

Jeanette went up to bed and I sat staring at the fire. We both felt enriched and fortunate, and here with each other in this getaway, unusually blessed. Yet we were daily being stretched beyond our limits. For me, no coasting was possible in CTI's burgeoning communications ministry. No letup for Jeanette, either. And if the demands now were great, what about getting these kids through adolescence in a culture that pitted children against parents? How would we handle identity crises and rebellion? Yes, we'd been there, done that—but this time around could bring problems so huge, they would be beyond our capacities.

I reached for some note cards I'd made during devotional times. Fénelon always seemed to have just the right insights: "Never say, 'This is all too much for me.' Depend on the Almighty. God's hand holds you. Do not try to look too far ahead, but live moment by moment before God. Let your anxiety flow away like a stream."

Once again Fénelon had nailed it. I flipped through a number of cards and saw that he repeatedly said that faith holds us in continual suspense, that we're "constantly up in the air." We must simply let God act and let his will unfold.

Actually, I'd experienced that, praying each day and watching events wonderfully unfold in ways I could never have engineered. If the Christian life was the magnificent adventure the Gospels describe, shouldn't I be filled with expectancy about what God was about to do next? Although I didn't like it one bit, big troubles were the essence of adventure.

I prayed for a continuing sense of wonder at God's "river glorious." In it I was being swirled around boulders and rushed into rapids and plunged down waterfalls—but what else did I expect? After all, prayer is dangerous. As Oswald Chambers said, when you pray your horizon is altered. Everything is in a new framework. You are compelled to act.

I stirred up the fire, then reached for a set of purple sheets called *Writers' Ink*. It was a student publication from Rick's school, and his essay "The Best Gift" had been selected for inclusion. More than once Jeanette and I had savored these affirming words from Rick.

"Of all the gifts I've ever received," it started, "the best one is the gift my parents gave me when I was adopted. Being adopted has provided me with a very loving and caring family. . . . Because of being adopted, I was given the gift of life, and to me that is the best gift anyone can receive." Rick's essay then sensitively explored why he had needed to be adopted and what his family, friends, teachers, and neighbors meant to him.

My eyes rested on this line: "My parents show me a ton of love and affection, and that is an important thing to know when you are growing up."

Indeed. It warmed me that he felt our love, especially since it was sometimes tough love. And I prayed that whatever he or his siblings might do or experience in the future, they'd all keep feeling that.

"The Best Gift." Maybe Rick's little school essay was the year's best gift to Jeanette and me.

Among my cards was also Eugene Peterson's paraphrase of Colossians 3:2, which I stared at as the last coals of the fire glowed red and hot: "Don't shuffle along, eyes to the ground, absorbed with the things right in front of you. Look up, and be alert to what is going on around Christ—that's where the action is. See things from his perspective."

dedication

First and foremost, for my wife, Jeanette, the driving force of love for our children. Her unsinkable tenacity and faith have kept us afloat in many tempests and storms.

For our parents, who modeled the naturalness of just responding to God when children are in need.

For Michelle, Todd, and Greg, who opened their rooms and hearts to little siblings and have loved them even when it was costly.

For the O'Hare skycap and many other African-Americans who have gone out of their way to smile at us and our black children and say, "Good for you!"

For the Badgeros, the Bedrossians, the Bells, the Dodds, Cindy Cronk, the Maxwells, the Penneys, and many others who have also adopted transracially. Their friendship creates strong, supportive networks for identity and faith.

Also, many thanks to Lyn Cryderman, whose suggestions and vision for the book shaped and refined it.

We want to hear from you. Please send your comments about this book to us in care of the address below. Thank you.

ZondervanPublishingHouse
Grand Rapids, Michigan 49530
http://www.zondervan.com